Guiding Those Left Behind In New Jersey

ALL THE LEGAL AND PRACTICAL THINGS
YOU NEED TO DO
TO SETTLE AN ESTATE IN NEW JERSEY
and
HOW TO ARRANGE YOUR OWN AFFAIRS
TO AVOID UNNECESSARY COSTS
TO YOUR FAMILY

BY AMELIA E. POHL, ESQ,
WITH
NEW JERSEY ATTORNEY BARRY E. LEVINE

EAGLE PUBLISHING COMPANY OF BOCA

The purpose of this book is to provide the reader with an accurate and informative overview of the subject but laws change frequently and are subject to different interpretations as courts rule on the meaning or effect of a law. This book is sold with the understanding that neither the publisher nor the authors are engaging in, nor rendering legal, medical, psychiatric, accounting or any other professional service. If you need legal, accounting, medical, psychiatric or other expert advice, then you should seek the services of a duly licensed professional.

WEB SITES: Web sites appear throughout the book. These Web sites are offered for the convenience of the reader only. Publication of these Web site addresses is not an endorsement by the authors, editors or publishers of this book.

This book is intended for use by the consumer for his or her own benefit. If you use this book to counsel someone about the law, accounting or medicine, then that may be considered an unauthorized and illegal practice.

EAGLE PUBLISHING COMPANY OF BOCA
4199 N. Dixie Highway, #2
Boca Raton, FL 33431
E-mail info@eaglepublishing.com

Printed in the United States of America
ISBN 1-892407-23-X
Library of Congress Catalog Card Number: 00-190355

The Organization of the Book

If you are going to GUIDE THOSE LEFT BEHIND, you need to know what is involved in settling an estate in New Jersey, so we begin the book explaining that process. The first six chapters explain:

1. How to tend to the funeral and burial
2. What agencies need to be notified of the death
3. How to locate the decedent's property
4. What bills need (and do not need) to be paid.
5. Determining who are the beneficiaries
6. Getting the decedent's property to the proper beneficiary

We devoted a chapter to each of these 6 steps; and for those who are in the process of settling an estate, we placed a CHECK LIST at the end of Chapter 6 to assist in remembering things that need to be done.

Once you read Chapters 1 through 6 you will be able to identify those problems that can occur when someone dies. Using those Chapters as a base, chapters 7 and 8 explain how to set up your own estate plan so that your family is not burdened by similar problems. Chapter 9 offers suggestions that you may find helpful if you or a member of your family are having difficulty getting through the grieving process.

GLOSSARY

This book is designed for the average reader. Legal terminology has been kept to a minimum. There is a glossary at the end of the book in the event you come across a legal term that is not familiar to you.

FICTITIOUS NAMES AND EVENTS

The examples in this book are based loosely on actual events; however, all names are fictitious; and the events, as portrayed, are fictitious.

About the Author

Before becoming an attorney in 1985, AMELIA E. POHL taught mathematics on both the high school and college level. During her tenure as Associate Professor of Mathematics at Prince George's Community College in Maryland, she wrote several books including Probability: A Set Theory Approach, Principals of Counting and Common Stock Sense.

During her practice of law Attorney Pohl observed that many people want to reduce the high cost of legal fees by performing or assisting with their own legal transactions. Attorney Pohl found that, with a bit of guidance, people are able to perform many legal transactions for themselves. Attorney Pohl utilizes her background as teacher, author and attorney to provide that "bit of guidance" to the general public in the form of self-help legal books that she has written. Attorney Pohl is currently "translating" this book for the remaining 49 states:

Guiding Those Left Behind in Alabama
Guiding Those Left Behind in Connecticut, etc.

Consulting New Jersey Attorney

BARRY E. LEVINE has been a member of the New Jersey Bar for over 25 years. He is a graduate of Rutgers College in New Brunswick, New Jersey. He received his Juris Doctor degree from the Rutgers School of Law in Camden, New Jersey.

Mr. Levine has extensive experience in the areas of Estate and Probate Law, Real Estate, Elder Law and Litigation. He has particular interest in assisting people with disabilities.

Among his many community activities, he has served as President and Legal Counsel to The ARC (formerly known as the Association for Retarded Citizens) Morris County Chapter, New Jersey.

Mr. Levine is in private practice in Morris Plains, New Jersey.

The Consulting Psychologist

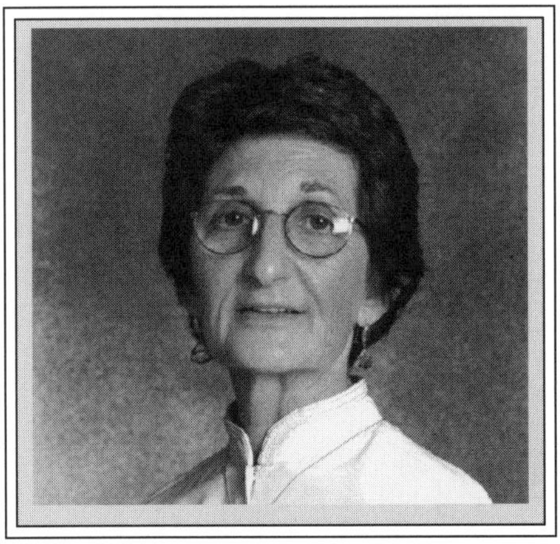

BARBARA J. SIMMONDS, Ph.D., a noted psychologist, collaborated with the author on Chapter 9 of this book which deals with the grieving process. Dr. Simmonds has been practicing in the field of Health/Rehabilitation Psychology and Gerontology for the past 10 years. Her experiences in the field led her as a natural outcome to develop expertise also in Grief Counseling, since so many losses accrue to individuals in a health care setting.

In addition to her work in hospitals, nursing centers and private practice, Dr. Simmonds has served as Adjunct Faculty at Nova Southeastern University, teaching courses in Aging, Stress Management and Grief Counseling. Dr. Simmonds holds a Master's Degree in Gerontology and a Ph.D. in Clinical Psychology from Nova Southeastern University. She was the Director of Psychological Services at Villa Maria Nursing and Rehabilitation Center for eight years and now continues her relationship with the institution on a consultation basis. She continues with her private practice in North Miami, Florida.

To my brother, Paul Adinolfi,
his intelligence, good humor and kindness,
his strength during our times of family loss,
have set the beacon standard for me to follow.

ACKNOWLEDGMENTS

When someone dies, the family attorney is often among the first to be called. Family members have questions about whether probate is necessary, who to notify, how to get possession of the assets, etc. Over the years, as we practiced in the field of Elder Law, we noticed that the questions raised were much the same family to family. We both agreed that a book answering such questions would be of service to the general public. We wish to thank all of the clients, whom we have had the honor and pleasure to serve, for providing us with the impetus to produce this book.

Special thanks from AMELIA E. POHL
I wish to express my sincere appreciation for the assistance and encouragement given to me by Martha Dermer, Michael J. DeMarie, CPA, my daughters Louise Lucas and Margot Bosche, and to my husband J. William Pohl.

Special thanks from BARRY E. LEVINE
I wish to than my wife, Elizabeth, and my children, Eric and Lauren, for their assistance and encouragement in the preparation of this book.

Guiding Those Left Behind In New Jersey

CONTENTS

About The Book

We tried to make this book as comprehensive as possible so there are specialized sections of the book that do not apply to the general population and may not be of interest to you. The following GUIDE POSTS appear throughout the book. You can read the section if the situation applies to you or skip the section if it doesn't.

GUIDE POSTS

SPOUSE

The SPOUSE POST means that the information provided is specifically for the spouse of the decedent. If the decedent was single, then skip this section.

LAWYER

The CALL-A-LAWYER POST alerts you to a situation that may require the assistance of an attorney. See page xiii for information about how to find a lawyer.

CAUTION

The CAUTION POST alerts you to a potential problem. It is followed by a suggestion about how to avoid the problem.

Special Situation

The SPECIAL SITUATION POST means that the information given in that paragraph applies to a particular event or situation; for example when someone dies a violent death. If the situation does not apply in your case then you can skip the section.

Reading the Law

Where applicable, we identified the state statute or federal statute that is the basis of the discussion. We did this as a reference, and also to encourage the general public to read the law as it is written. Prior to the Internet the only way you could look up the law was to physically take yourself to the local courthouse law library or the law section of a public library. Today all of the state and federal statutes are literally at your finger tips. They are just a mouse click away on the Internet. All you need to look up the law is the address of the Web site and the identifying number of the statute.

New Jersey statutes are divided into Titles numbered from 1 to 59; for example Taxation is Title 54. Some Titles have a letter as well as a number. For example, Insurance is Title 17BA. Each Title is divided into chapters and each chapter into sections. We will refer to the statute by identifying the number of the Title and the chapter and section within that Title. For example, the notation (NJ 3B:8-7) refers to Title 3B (Administration of Estates), Chapter 8, section 7. You can find the statute by looking at the table of contents at the New Jersey Statute Web site:

NEW JERSEY STATUTE WEB SITE
http://www.njleg.state.nj.us

To locate Federal statutes, you can refer to the table of contents at the Federal Statute Web site:

FEDERAL STATUTE WEB SITE
http://www4.law.cornell.edu/uscode

If you come across a topic that is of importance to you, then you may find it both interesting and profitable to actually read the law as written.

When You Need A Lawyer

This book describes New Jersey law as in effect when the book was written. We pay our legislators (state and federal) to make laws and, if necessary, change those in effect. We pay judges to interpret the law and that interpretation may change the way the law operates. The legislature and the judiciary do their job and so laws change frequently.

The purpose of the book is to give the reader an overview of what needs to be done when someone dies, and to provide information about how a person can arrange his own affairs to avoid problems for his own family. It is not intended as a substitute for legal counsel or any other kind of professional advice. If you have any legal question, then you should seek the counsel of an attorney. When looking for an attorney, consider three things:

EXPERTISE, COST and PERSONALITY.

EXPERTISE

The State Bar of New Jersey has legal specialist programs for four areas of practice: Civil, Criminal; Matrimonial; and Worker's Compensation. To be a "certified specialist" in any of the above areas of law, the attorney must pass a written examination, have at least 5 years experience in that area of the law. In addition they need to fulfill ongoing education requirements to keep up with changes in the law.

You can call the New Jersey State Bar Association at (732) 249-5000 for information about how to reach an attorney who is experienced in the area of law that you seek. The New Jersey State Bar Association has a Web Site that offers a list of Lawyer Referral Services::

NEW JERSEY STATE BAR ASSOCIATION
http://www.njlsba.com

Certification is just one of the criteria to consider. Many fine attorneys are experienced in an area of law, but have not taken the time, effort and expense to become certified as a specialist in that area of law by the New Jersey Bar. If the attorney is not certified in the branch of law that you need, then ask how long he has practiced that type of law and what percentage of his practice is devoted to that type of law.

Of course, the best way to find an attorney is through personal referral. Ask your friends, family or business acquaintances if they have used an attorney for the field of law that you seek and whether they were pleased with the results. It is important to employ an attorney who is experienced in the kind of law you seek. Your friend may have a wonderful Estate Planning attorney, but if you have suffered an injury, then you need a Personal Injury attorney.

COST

In addition to the attorney's experience, it is important that you check out what you can expect to pay in attorney's fees. When you call for an appointment ask what the attorney will charge for the initial consultation and the approximate cost for the service you seek. Ask whether there will be any additional costs such as filing fees, accounting fees, expert witness fees, etc.

If the least expensive attorney is out of your price range then there are many state and private agencies throughout the state that provide legal assistance for people of low income. Some of the agencies are as follows:

Legal Services of New Jersey, Inc. Edison, NJ	(732) 572-9100
Bergen County Legal Services Private Attorney Involvement Program	(201) 487-2166
Essex-Newark Legal Services Project, Inc. Volunteer Lawyers Project	(973) 624-4500
Monmouth County Legal Aid Society, Inc.	(908) 776-7733

You can call your local County Bar Association for the telephone number of the Legal Services office nearest you.

The American Bar Association has a Web site that lists telephone numbers for New Jersey state Legal Pro Bono Programs:

AMERICAN BAR ASSOCIATION WEB SITE
www.abanet.org/legalservices/probono/pb-newjersey

PERSONALITY

Of equal importance to the attorney's experience and legal fees, is your relationship with the attorney. How easy was it to reach the attorney? Did you go through layers of receptionists and legal assistants before being allowed to speak to the attorney? Did the attorney promptly return your call? If you had difficulty reaching the attorney, then you can expect similar problems should you employ that attorney.

Did the attorney treat you with respect? Did the attorney treat you paternally with a "father knows best" attitude or did the attorney treat you as an intelligent person with the ability to understand the options available to you and the ability to make your own decision based on the information provided to you.

Are you able to understand and easily communicate with the attorney? Is he/she speaking to you in plain English or is his/her explanation of the matter so full of legalese to be almost meaningless to you?

Do you find the attorney's personality to be pleasant or grating? Sometimes people rub each other the wrong way. It is like rubbing a cat the wrong way. Stroking a cat from head to tail is pleasing to the cat, but petting it in the opposite direction, no matter how well intended, causes friction. If the lawyer makes you feel annoyed or uncomfortable then find another attorney.

It is worth the effort to take the time to interview as many attorneys as it takes to find one with the right expertise, fee schedule and personality for you.

1 The First Week

Dealing with the death of a close family member or friend is difficult. Not only do you need to deal with your own emotions, but often with those of your family and friends. Sometimes their sorrow is more painful to you, than what you are experiencing yourself.

In addition to the emotional impact of a death, there are many things that need to be done, from arranging the funeral and burial, to closing out the business affairs of the decedent, and finally giving whatever property is left to the proper beneficiary.

The funeral and burial take only a few days. Wrapping up the affairs of the *decedent* (the person who died) may take considerably longer. This chapter explains what things you (the spouse or closest family member) need to do during the first week, beginning at the moment of death and continuing through the funeral.

♀ MALE GENDER USED ♂

Rather than use "he/she" or "his/her" for simplicity (and hoping not to offend anyone) we will refer to the decedent and his Personal Representative using the male gender.

References to other people will be in both genders.

AUTOPSIES

In today's high tech world of medicine, doctors are fairly certain of the cause of death, but if there is a question, the family should consider having an autopsy performed. To do the examination, written permission must be obtained from any of the following persons who have assumed responsibility of the body for burial: spouse, adult child, parent, or other next of kin. If more than one person has taken custody of the body for burial, then only one person need agree to the examination. If no relative can be reached, then anyone who has the legal duty to bury the body may give consent for an autopsy (NJ 26:6-50).

The cost of an autopsy runs anywhere from several hundred to over three thousand dollars. The person giving authorization must agree to pay for the autopsy because the cost is not covered under most health insurance plans. It is in the family's best interest to consent to the autopsy. The examination might reveal a genetic disorder, that could be treated if it later appears in another family member. The family member may have died because of incorrect medical treatment or perhaps foul play. Even if no such cause is found, knowing the cause of death with certainty is better than not knowing.

That was the case with the family of a woman who was taken to the hospital complaining of stomach pains. The doctors thought she might be suffering from gallbladder disease but she died before they could effectively treat her. A doctor suggested that an autopsy be performed to determine the actual cause of death. The woman had three daughters, one of whom objected to the autopsy "Why spend that kind of money?
It won't bring Mom back."

The daughter's wishes were respected and no autopsy was performed. However, over the years, as each of the daughters aged and became ill with their own various ailments they would undergo physical examinations. As part of taking their medical history, doctors would routinely ask "And what was cause of your mother's death?" None could answer the question.

This is not a dramatic story. No mysterious genetic disorder ever occurred in any of her daughters, nor in any of their children. But each daughter (including the one who objected) at some point in her life, was confronted with the nagging question "What did Mom die of?"

MANDATORY AUTOPSIES

When a person dies, a physician must sign the death certificate stating the cause of death. If a person dies in a hospital, then there is a doctor present to sign the certificate. If a person dies at home then the police must be notified. The person who discovers the body needs to call 911. The police will have the medical examiner determine the cause of death. If the death was from a disease that might pose a threat to the public health or if the death was not from natural causes, then the medical examiner, or county prosecutor or a superior court judge can order an autopsy to be performed. Autopsies so ordered are paid for by the state (NJ 52:17B-88).

AUTOPSIES PERFORMED BY THE INSURANCE COMPANY:

A company that issues an accident or health insurance policy in New Jersey is required to include a statement in the policy that the company has the right to perform an autopsy. The cost of the autopsy is paid for by the insurance company, so they will not order an autopsy unless there is some important reason to do so (NJ 17B:26-13).

If, before death, the decedent made an anatomical gift by signing a donor card, then hospital personnel or the donor's doctor needs to be made aware of the gift in quick proximity to the time of death — preferably before death.

GIFT AUTHORIZED BY THE FAMILY

Hospital personnel determine whether a mortally ill patient is a candidate for an organ donation. Early on in the donor program those over 65 were not considered as suitable candidates. Today, however, the condition of the organ, and not the age, is the determining factor.

The federal government has established regional Organ Procurement Organizations throughout the United States, to coordinate the donor program. The Organ Procurement Organization for the state of New Jersey is located in Springfield. It is called the New Jersey Organ and Tissue Sharing Network. If it is decided that the patient is a candidate, the hospital will contact the Organ Procurement Organization.

The Organ Procurement Organization will determine whether the patient is a suitable donor. If they decide to request the gift and the candidate did not sign a donor card then someone in the family must give written permission. Someone who is specially trained will approach the family to request the donation. New Jersey statute 26:6-58 establishes an order of priority to authorize the donation:

- 1st the spouse
- 2nd an adult son or daughter
- 3rd either parent
- 4th an adult brother or sister
- 5th the decedent's court appointed guardian of his person
- 6th anyone authorized to dispose of the body

If permission is obtained from a family member and there are others in the same or a higher priority, then an effort must be made to contact those people and make them aware of the proposed gift. For example, if the sister of the decedent agrees to the gift (4th in priority) and the decedent had an adult child (2nd in priority), then the child needs to be made aware of the gift. If the child objects, then no gift can be made. Similarly, the statute prohibits the gift if the decedent ever expressed his opposition to a donation.

AFTER THE DONATION

If the family agrees to the donation, then once the operation is complete the body is delivered to the funeral home and prepared for burial or cremation as directed by the family. The operation does not disfigure the body so there can be an open casket viewing if the family so wishes.

Once the donation is made, the Organ Procurement Organization keeps in touch with the donor's family. If the family wishes they will provide them with basic demographic information about the donation, such as the age, sex, marital status, number of children and occupation of the recipient of the gift.

If the recipient of the gift wishes to write to the donor's family to thank them for the gift, the Organ Procurement Organization will contact the donor's family and ask if they wish to receive the letter. If not, then the letter is kept on file in the event that the donor's family may want to read it at a later date.

GIFT FOR EDUCATION OR RESEARCH

If the decedent signed a donor card indicating his wish to use his body for any purpose and he is not a candidate for an organ donation, then you can offer to release the body to either of the following institutions to be used for education or research:

University of Medicine and Dentistry of New Jersey
Department of Anatomy
185 South Orange Avenue
Newark, NJ 07103
(973) 972-4648

Robert Wood Johnson Anatomical Association
675 Hoes Lane
Piscataway, NJ 08854-5635
(800) 443-8211

You will need to call the facility within 24 hours to determine whether they will accept the body. Most schools will not accept bodies from those who have died from a contagious disease or from crushing injuries. If they accept the donation, they will charge a transportation fee to deliver the body to the school. The fee is based on the distance traveled and usually is under $300.

The study can take up to 2 years to complete. Once finished, the remains are cremated and the institution will have the ashes buried in a local cemetery. If the family wishes, the ***cremains*** (cremated remains) will be returned to them for a shipping fee of $25.

CAVEAT: It is illegal for anyone to purchase body parts. It is legal to charge monies to prepare or transport bodies or body parts. Not-for profit and as well as for-profit companies have sprung up that are in the business of preparing and delivering body parts. These companies request donations from families (so they are not buying body parts). The company prepares the body tissue or other parts of the body, and then distributes the parts throughout the United States to physicians, hospitals, research centers, etc. In many cases the monies charged for preparation and transportation includes a sizable profit. If someone other than your local Organ Procurement Organization (as identified on page 4) approaches you to make a donation, then before making the donation you may want to:

LEARN ABOUT THE COMPANY

You may want to learn about the company requesting the donation:

What is the name of the company?
Where are their main headquarters located?
What is their primary business activity?
What is the name and job description of the person making the request?

DETERMINE THE END USE OF THE DONATION

You may want to ask what they intend to do with the tissue or body part. If it is being used for research, then what type of research? Where is the research being conducted? If it will be used for transplantation, then what agency (doctor, hospital) will receive the donation and where is that agency located?

THE FUNERAL

Approximately ten percent of all deaths occur suddenly because of an accident, suicide, foul play or undetected illness. But most deaths are anticipated with the common scenario being that of a person dying after being ill for many months. Expected or not, the first job is the disposition of the body.

THE PREARRANGED FUNERAL

Increasingly, people are making advance arrangements for their own funeral and burial. This makes it easier on the family both financially and emotionally. All decisions have been made and there is no guessing what the decedent would have wanted.

If the decedent made provision for his burial space, then you need to locate the burial certificate. If the decedent purchased a preneed funeral plan, then you need to locate the contract. You should read the contract to determine what provisions were made. Some contracts are paid on an installment basis. If the decedent signed such a contract, then you need to find out what monies were paid and whether there is a remaining balance due.

If you cannot locate the contract, but you know the name of the funeral home, then call and ask them to send you a copy of the contract. If you believe the decedent purchased a funeral plan but you do not know the name of the funeral home, then call the local funeral homes. Many local funeral homes are owned by national firms with computer capacity to identify people who have purchased a contract in any of their many locations.

Once you have possession of the contract, bring it with you to the funeral home and go over the terms of the contract with the funeral director. Inquire whether there is any charge that is not included in the contract.

MAKING FUNERAL ARRANGEMENTS

If the decedent died unexpectedly or without having made any prior funeral arrangements, then your first job is to choose a funeral director and make arrangements for the funeral or cremation. Most people choose the nearest or most conveniently located funeral home without comparison shopping, however prices for these services can vary significantly from funeral home to funeral home. Savings can be had if you take the time to make a few phone calls.

Receiving price quotes by telephone is your right under Federal law. Federal Trade Commission ("FTC") Rule 453.2 (b) (1) requires a funeral director to give an accurate telephone quote of the prices of his goods and services. Funeral homes are listed in the telephone directory under FUNERAL DIRECTORS. If you live in a small town, there may be only one or two listings. If such is the case, then check out some funeral homes in the next largest city.

Funeral Directors usually provide the following services:

- obtain burial and transit permits
- arrange for the transportation of the body to the funeral home and then to the burial site
- arrange for the embalming or cremation of the body
- arrange funeral and memorial services
- file the death certificate and order copies for the family
- have memorial and acknowledgment cards printed
- arrange to print the obituary

To compare prices you will need to determine:

- ✧ what is included in the price of a basic funeral plan
- ✧ whether you can expect any additional cost.

Embalming may be necessary if you are going to have a viewing. Embalming is not necessary if you order a direct cremation or an immediate burial. Federal Trade Commission Rule 453.5 prohibits the funeral home from charging an embalming fee unless you order the service.

If the decedent did not own a burial space, then that cost must be included when making funeral arrangements.

PURCHASING THE CASKET

When comparison-shopping, you will find that the single most expensive item in the funeral arrangement is the casket. Most funeral directors will quote you a price for the basic funeral plan. That plan does not include the cost of the casket. Directors usually quote a range of prices for the casket, saying that you will need to come in and choose the casket at the time you contract for the funeral.

When selecting a casket you should be aware that there is a considerable markup in the price quoted by the funeral director. You do not need to deal "sole source" when purchasing a the casket. You can purchase a casket elsewhere and have it delivered to the funeral home for use instead of the one offered by the funeral director.

In 1994, The Federal Trade Commission ruled that funeral homes had to accept caskets purchased elsewhere. (FTC Rule 453.4). The ruling includes a ban on funeral homes charging a handling fee for accepting a casket purchased elsewhere.

If you wish to shop for a casket, then the best time to do so is before you go to the funeral home to arrange for the funeral. You can find a retail casket sales outlet in the telephone book under CASKETS. You may need to look in the telephone directory for the nearest large city to find a listing. For users of the Internet, you can use your search engine to find the retail sales casket company nearest you. By making a call to a retail casket sales dealer, you will become knowledgeable in the price range of caskets. You can then decide what is a reasonable price for the product you seek.

Once you have determined what you should pay for the casket, it is only fair to give the funeral director the opportunity to meet that price. If you cannot reach a meeting of the minds, then you can always order the casket from the retail sales dealer and have it delivered to the funeral home.

ON-LINE FUNERAL SERVICES

The Internet is changing the way the world does business, and the funeral industry is no exception. A growing number of mortuaries are offering live Webcasts of funerals and wakes for those who are unable to pay their respects in person.

There are Web sites such as ObitDetails.com where you can post an obituary. There are online memorial chat rooms as well as online eulogies and testimonials. There is even a Web site that offers a posthumous e-mail service so that people can leave a final message for their friends and relatives.

THE CREMATION

Increasingly people are opting for cremation. The reasons for choosing cremation are varied, but for the majority, it is a matter of finances. The cost of cremation is approximately one-sixth that of an ordinary funeral and burial. A major saving is the cost of the casket. No casket is necessary for the cremation. Federal law prohibits a Funeral Director from saying that a casket is required for a direct cremation (FTC Rule 453.3 (b)ii). Of course if you want to have a viewing of the body and/or a funeral service with the body present, then you may need to purchase a disposable casket made of wood or cardboard, or you can rent a casket from the Funeral Director.

If you are having a memorial service in a place of worship with no viewing of the body before the cremation, then consider contracting with a facility that does cremations only. Look in the telephone book under CREMATION SERVICES. You will also see cremation "societies" in the telephone book. Some are for-profit and others not-for-profit. You can also find advertisements for cremation services on the Internet. These cremation facilities provide much the same services as a funeral home but with one important exception — the cremation service does not provide any type of funeral service or public viewing of the body.

Special Situation THE OVERWEIGHT DECEDENT

If the decedent weighs more than 300 pounds, then you need to check to see if the Cremation service has facilities large enough to handle the body. If you cannot locate a crematory that can accommodate the body, then you need to make burial arrangements.

DISPOSING OF THE ASHES

The decedent's cremains can be placed in a cemetery. Many cemeteries have a separate building called a ***columbarium***, which is especially designed to store urns. If not, then the cremains can be placed in a cemetery plot. Some cemeteries allow the cremains of a family member to be placed in a occupied family plot. Similarly, some cemeteries will allow the cremains to be place in the space in a mausoleum that is currently occupied by a member of the decedent's family. If it is your desire to have the cremains placed in an occupied mausoleum or family plot, then you need to call the cemetery and ask them to explain their policy as it relates to the burial of urns in occupied sites.

If the cremains are to be placed in a cemetery, then you need to obtain a suitable urn for the burial. You can purchase the urn from the Funeral Director or Crematory Service Director. Urns cost much less than caskets, but they can cost several hundred dollars. You may wish to do some comparison shopping by calling a retail sales casket dealer.

The decedent may have expressed a desire that his ashes be spread out to sea. The Funeral Director or Cremation Service Director can assist you with such arrangements, or you can do so yourself.

SPOUSE

THE MILITARY BURIAL

Subject to availability of burial spaces, an honorably discharged veteran and/or his unmarried minor or handicapped child and/or his un-remarried spouse may be buried in a military cemetery. There are two national cemeteries located in New Jersey:
The Beverly National Cemetery; Beverly, NJ 08010
Finn's Point National Cemetery; Salem, NJ 08079
These sites have room for cremains. For information call (609) 877-5460.

There are two state Veterans cemeteries that currently have space for veterans who established residency in New Jersey prior to their death:

Brigadier General William C. Doyle
Veterans Memorial Cemetery
350 Provinceline Road, Route #2
Wrightstown, NJ 08562
(609) 758-7250

New Jersey Memorial Home Cemetery
524 N.W. Boulevard
Vineland, NJ 08360
(609) 696-6350

The Department of the Army is in charge of the Arlington National Cemetery. If you wish to have an eligible deceased veteran buried in the Arlington National Cemetery, then call them at (703) 695-3250:

Arlington National Cemetery
Interment Service Branch
Arlington, VA 22211

Special Situation

THE COST OF A MILITARY BURIAL

Burial space in a National Cemetery is free of charge. Cemetery employees will open and close the grave and mark it with headstone or grave marker without cost to the family. The local Veteran's Administration ("VA") will provide the family with a memorial flag. The family needs to make funeral arrangements with a funeral firm and have them transport the remains to the cemetery.

If the decedent was receiving a VA pension then the VA will pay a burial and funeral expense allowance regardless of where the veteran is buried. The VA will not reimburse any burial or funeral cost for the spouse of a veteran.

For information about reimbursement of funeral and burial expenses you can call the VA at (800) 827-1000.

The Department of Veteran's Affairs has a Web site with information on the following topics:

- National and Military Cemeteries
- Burial, Headstones and Markers
- State Cemetery Grants Program
- Obtaining Military Records
- Locating Veterans

VA CEMETERY WEB SITE
http://www.cem.va.gov

SPOUSE

BENEFITS FOR SPOUSE OF DECEDENT VETERAN

If the decedent was honorably discharged, then regardless of where he is buried, his spouse might be eligible for a contribution from the Veteran's Administration for his funeral and burial expenses. If the decedent had minor or disabled children, his spouse may also be eligible for a monthly benefit of Dependency and Indemnity Compensation ("DIC").

If the Veteran's surviving spouse receives nursing home care under Medicaid, then the spouse might be eligible for a monthly payment from the VA. Whether the surviving spouse is eligible for any of these benefits depends on many factors including whether the decedent was serving on active duty, whether his death was service related, and the surviving spouse's assets and income.

For information about whether the surviving spouse is eligible for any benefit related to the decedent's military service, call the VETERANS ADMINISTRATION at (800) 827-1000.

You can receive a printed statement of public policy: VA Pamphlet 051-000-00217-2 FEDERAL BENEFITS FOR VETERANS AND DEPENDENTS by sending a check in the amount of $5 to:

THE SUPERINTENDENT OF DOCUMENTS
P.O. Box 371954
Pittsburgh, PA 15250-7954

Information is also available on the VA web site:

VA WEB SITE
http://www.va.gov

Special Situation

THE PROBLEM FUNERAL OR BURIAL

The funeral and burial industry is well regulated by the state and federal government. The following are some of the things that are prohibited:

- ⌧ Soliciting business from one about to die or from a family who has just suffered a loss (NJ 45:7-65.3)
- ⌧ Serving any food or refreshment in conjunction with any funeral (NJ 45:7-65.1)
- ⌧ Representing that a casket is required for a direct cremation (FTC Rule 453.3 (b) 1)
- ⌧ Neglecting to give a printed price list of their caskets at the beginning of the discussion and before showing the caskets. (FTC Rule 453.2 (b)2)

Funeral directors are licensed professionals so it is unusual to have a problem with the funeral or burial or cremation. If, however, you had a bad experience with any aspect of the funeral then you can file a complaint with the New Jersey state licensing agency:

State Board of Mortuary Science
P.O. Box 45009
Newark, NJ 07101
Telephone: (973) 504-6425

☎ LAWYER

In addition to filing a complaint with the Board, you may wish to consult with an attorney who is experienced in litigation matters to learn of any other legal remedy that you may have.

Special Situation

THE OUT OF STATE BURIAL

If the decedent is to be buried in another state, then the body will need to be transported to that state. Most funeral firms belong to a national network of funeral firms, and the out-of-state funeral director has the means to make local arrangements to ship the body. Contact the out-of-state funeral director and have him/her make arrangement with the airline for the transportation of the body.

If services are to be held in New Jersey and in another state, then contact the local funeral firm and they will make arrangements with the out-of-state funeral firm to transport the body.

If the body has been cremated, then you can transport the ashes yourself, either by carrying the ashes as part of your luggage or by arranging with the airline to transport the ashes as cargo. You should have a certified copy of the death certificate available in the event that you need to identify the cremains of the decedent. Call the airline before departure and ask whether they have any special regulation or procedure regarding the transportation of human ashes.

Special Situation

THE UNCLAIMED BODY

Each municipality is charged with the duty of disposing of the remains of the indigent or unidentified decedent. If a person is receiving old-age assistance dies without sufficient funds for burial, and there is no one willing to pay for the burial, then the County Welfare Agency will do so. Similarly, if a person dies of natural causes and the identity of the person cannot be determined, the Director of Welfare, under the direction of the County Welfare Board will employ someone to supervise the burial in the county cemetery. If there is no county cemetery, then the County Welfare Board will contract with a local cemetery to bury the indigent. (NJ 44:1-157, 44:4-118, 44:7-13).

If an indigent person dies and the police can determine his identity, they will try to locate the family. If the decedent was an honorably discharged veteran, then the Veteran's Administration will arrange for a burial (see page 15). If the decedent was not an honorably discharged veteran and his family is unable or unwilling to make burial arrangements, the Director of Welfare will arrange for an indigent burial in the county of the decedent's residence or the county where the death occurred.

Special Situation

THE VIOLENT DEATH

If the decedent died a violent death or under circumstances in which foul play is suspected, the Medical Examiner will take possession of the body. The body will not be released to the funeral director until the examination of the body is complete. In the interim, the family can proceed with arrangements for the funeral. The funeral director will contact the Medical Examiner to determine when he can pick up the body and proceed with the funeral.

If the decedent died because of a criminal act and you are a family member, then you may wish to contact an attorney experienced in Criminal Law to learn of your rights as a family member. If the perpetrator of the crime has significant funds, you may want to sue him/her for the wrongful death.

☎ LAWYER

THE ACCIDENTAL DEATH

If the decedent died because of an accident, then it is important to contact a Personal Injury attorney to determine whether the family has a case for wrongful death. If the accident was related to the decedent's job, the family may wish to consult with a Worker's Compensation attorney as well.

Special Situation

CRIME VICTIM COMPENSATION

If the decedent died because of a criminal act and you are a family member or the sexual partner of the decedent, then you may be eligible to receive compensation under the CRIME INJURIES COMPENSATION ACT. The state can provide compensation for reasonable funeral expenses and for medical care for up to $25,000. To be eligible the following must be true:

- The decedent was an innocent victim (i.e., did not do anything wrong).
- The crime was reported to authorities within 72 hours of its commission or discovery of the body.
- Application for compensation was filed within two year from the date of the crime.
- There are no other resources, such as health or life insurance, available to cover medical or burial costs.

The Victim Crimes Compensation Board will conduct an investigation to determine eligibility. You can be represented by an attorney. The state will pay for attorney's fees up to 15% of whatever amount is awarded. It is unlawful for the attorney to receive any money in excess of that amount. The process can take 6 months. If the Board determines that emergency funds are needed (for example, to pay for the burial), they can release up to $1,500. Whatever amount is awarded as emergency funds will be deducted from the final award (NJ 52:4B-1, 52:4B-2, 52:4B-8, 52:4B-10.1, 52:4B-18, 52:4B-22).

You can pick up an application form from any municipal police department or you can call the Victim Crimes Compensation Board at (609) 292-8446 and they will mail one to you.

☎ LAWYER THE MISSING BODY

Few things are more difficult to deal with than a missing person. The emotional turmoil created by the "not knowing" is often more difficult than the finality of death. The legal problems created by the disappearance are also more difficult than if the person simply died. It may take a two-part legal procedure; first to appoint someone to handle the missing persons affairs; and then a probate procedure if it is determined that the missing person is dead.

APPOINTING A TRUSTEE

If a person is missing and cannot be found after a diligent search, then that person is referred to as an ***absentee***. If the absentee has business matters that need attending (bills that need to be paid, checks that need to be cashed, etc.), then you can ***petition*** (ask) the Superior Court to appoint a Trustee to handle the absentee's affairs. You will need to employ an attorney who is experienced in probate matters in order to get the Trustee appointed (NJ 3B:26-2).

If the circumstances of the disappearance are sufficient to justify the belief that the missing person is dead or after 5 years have passed, whichever is earlier, the judge will issue an order stating that it is presumed that the mission person is dead. Once the court makes that determination, the probate procedure can begin (NJ 3B:27-1, 3B:27-6).

THE DEATH CERTIFICATE

The Funeral Director or Cremation Service Director will order as many certified copies of the death certificate as you request. Most establishments require an original certified copy and not a photocopy so you need to order sufficient copies.

The following is a list of institutions that may want a certified copy:

- Each insurance company that insured the decedent or his property (health insurance company, life insurance company, car insurance company, home insurance company)
- Each financial institution in which the decedent had money invested (brokerage houses, banks)
- The decedent's pension fund
- Each credit card company used by the decedent
- The IRS
- The Social Security Administration
- The Surrogate's Court in the county where the probate is conducted.

Some airlines and car rental companies offer a discount for short notice, emergency trips. If you have family flying in for the funeral, you may wish to order a few extra copies of the death certificate so that they can obtain an airline or car rental discount.

ORDERING COPIES OF THE DEATH CERTIFICATE

If you wish to order certified copies of the death certificate at a later date, you can call the funeral director and ask him to do so or you can write to:

New Jersey Department of Health and Senior Services
Bureau of Vital Statistics
P.O. Box 370
Trenton, NJ 08625-0370
Telephone: (609) 292-4087 Fax: (609) 392-4292

The present charge is $4 for each certified copy. They accept personal checks made payable to the New Jersey State Department of Health. It may take the Bureau up to 4 months to process your request, so you may first want to call and ask what information they require.

You can Fax your request to them and pay by credit card. The charge is $8.95 per certified copy, but the benefit is that they will process your request within 7 business days. For more information about faxing your request, call Vitalchek at (609) 633-2860.

About Probate

Once a person dies, all of the property he owns as of the date of his death is referred to as the ***Decedent's Estate.*** If the decedent owned property that was in his name only (not jointly or in trust for someone), then some sort of court procedure is necessary to determine who is entitled to possession of the property. The name of the court procedure is ***Probate.*** In New Jersey, probate is conducted in the Surrogates' Court in the county of the decedent's resident. In some counties probate is conducted in the Probate section of the Superior Court. For simplicity, we will refer to the Surrogates' Court when discussing the probate procedure, understanding that in some counties, probate is conducted in the Superior Court.

The root of the word probate is "to prove." It refers to the first job of the court, namely, to examine proof of whether the decedent died ***testate*** (with a valid Will) or ***intestate*** (without a valid Will). The second job of the court is to appoint someone to wrap up the affairs of the decedent — to pay any outstanding bills and then to distribute what property is left to the beneficiaries.

If the decedent named someone in his Will to be the ***Executor*** of his estate, then the Surrogates' court will appoint that person for the job and issue ***Letters Testamentary*** giving him authority to administer the estate. If the decedent died intestate, then the court will appoint someone to be the ***Administrator*** of the estate and issue ***Letters of Administration.*** For simplicity, we will use that term ***Personal Representative*** to represent anyone who has the job of settling the decedent's estate and the term ***Letters*** as the document that gives the Personal Representative authority to act (NJ 3B:1-1, 3B:10-1).

There are different ways to conduct a probate procedure depending on the value of the probate estate and whether the decedent owned real property at the time of his death. The method of conducting a probate procedure is called the ***estate administration***. Chapter 6 explains how to determine whether a probate procedure is necessary and if so, then what kind of administration is necessary.

But there are many things to consider before we discuss Probate, such as notifying everyone of the death and that is the topic of the next chapter.

Giving Notice Of The Death 2

Those closest to the decedent usually notify family members and close friends by telephone. The funeral director will arrange to have an obituary published in as many different newspapers as the family requests, but there is still the job of notifying the government and people who were doing business with the decedent. That task belongs to the person named as the Executor in the decedent's Will. If the decedent died without a Will, then the spouse the right to be appointed as Personal Representative. If there is no spouse, or if the spouse is unable or unwilling to serve, then anyone who has the right to inherit the decedent's property can be appointed. If there is a need to conduct a probate procedure and no heirs come forward within 40 days of the death, then the Surrogates' court will appoint any fit person to do the job (NJ 3B:10-2)

If no probate procedure is necessary, then the job of notifying people of the death and settling the decedent's affairs falls to his spouse; and in the absence of a spouse, to the decedent's next of kin. By ***next of kin,*** we mean those people who inherit the decedent's property according to the NEW JERSEY INTESTATE SUCCESSION ACT. That law is explained in Chapter 5.

The person who has the job of settling the decedent's estate should begin to give notice as soon as is practicable after the death. Two government agencies that need to be notified are the Social Security Administration and the IRS. This chapter gives their telephone number as well as those of all the other agencies that need to be notified.

NOTIFYING SOCIAL SECURITY

Many Funeral Directors will, as part of their service package, notify the Social Security Administration of the death. You may wish to check to see that this has been done. You can do so by calling (800) 772-1213. If you are hearing impaired call (800) 325-0778 TTY. You will need to give the Social Security Administration the full legal name of the decedent as well as his social security number and date of birth.

Special Situation

DECEDENT RECEIVING SOCIAL SECURITY CHECKS

If the decedent was receiving checks from Social Security, then you need to determine whether his last check needs to be returned to the Social Security Administration. Each Social Security check is a payment for the prior month, provided that person lives for the entire prior month. If someone dies on the last day of the month, then you should not cash the check for that month. For example, if someone dies on July 31st, then you need to return the check that the agency mails out in August. If however, the decedent died on August 1st then the check sent in August need not be returned because that check is payment for the month of July.

If the Social Security check is electronically deposited into a bank account then notify the bank that the account holder died and notify the Social Security Administration as well. If the check needs to be returned, then the Social Security Administration will withdraw it electronically from the bank account. You will need to keep the account open until the funds are withdrawn.

SPOUSE

SPOUSE/CHILD'S SOCIAL SECURITY BENEFITS

If the decedent had sufficient work credits, the Social Security Administration will give the decedent's widow(er) or if unmarried, then the decedent's minor children, a one-time death benefit in the amount of $255.

SURVIVORS BENEFITS:

The spouse (or ex-spouse) of the decedent may be eligible for Survivors Benefits. Benefits vary depending on the amount of work credits earned by the decedent; whether the decedent had minor or disabled children; the spouse's age; how long they were married; etc.

The minor child of the decedent may be eligible for dependent child's benefits regardless of whether the decedent father ever married the child's mother. Paternity can be established by any one of several methods including the father acknowledging his child in writing or verbally to members of his family.

SOCIAL SECURITY BENEFITS

A spouse or ex-spouse can collect social security benefits based on the decedent's work record. This value may be greater than the spouse now receives. It is important to make an appointment with your local Social Security office and determine whether you as the spouse (or ex-spouse) or parent of decedent's minor child are eligible for any Social Security or Survivor benefit. The Social Security Administration has a web site from which you can down load publications that explain survivors benefits:

SOCIAL SECURITY WEB SITE
http://www.ssa.gov

Special Situation

DECEDENT WITH GOVERNMENT PENSION

If the decedent was a federal retiree and received a government pension then any check received after the date of death needs to be returned to the U.S. Treasury. If the check is direct deposited to a bank account, then call the financial institution and ask them to return the check. If the check is sent by mail then you need to return it to: Director, Regional Finance Center

U. S. Treasury Department
P.O. Box 7367
Chicago, IL 60680

Include a letter explaining the reason for the return of the check and stating the decedent's date of death.

$$$ APPLY FOR BENEFITS $$$

Even though you notify the government of the death, they will not automatically give you benefits to which you may be entitled. You need to apply for those benefits by notifying the Office of Personnel Management ("OPM") of the death and requesting that they send you an application for survivor benefits. You can call them at (888) 767-6738 or you can write to:

THE OFFICE OF PERSONNEL MANAGEMENT
SERVICE AND RECORDS CENTER
BOYERS, PA 16017

You will find brochures and information about Survivor's Benefits at the OPM Web site:

OFFICE OF PERSONNEL MANAGEMENT WEB SITE
http://www.opm.gov
You can get assistance via E-mail at
retire@opm.gov

Special Situation

DECEDENT WITH COMPANY PENSION OR ANNUITY

In most cases, pension and annuity checks are payment for the prior month. If the decedent received his pension or annuity check before his death, then no monies need be returned. Pension checks and/or annuity checks received after the date of death may need to be returned to the company. You need to notify the company of the death to determine the status of the last check sent to the decedent.

Before notifying the company, locate the policy or pension statement that is the basis of the income. That document should tell whether there is a beneficiary of the pension or annuity funds now that the pensioner or annuitant is dead. If you cannot locate the document, use the return address on the check envelope and ask the company to send you a copy of the plan. Also request that they forward to you any claim form that may be required in order for the survivor or beneficiary to receive benefits under that pension plan or policy.

If the pension/annuity check is direct deposited to the decedent's account, then ask the bank to assist you in locating the company and notifying the company of the death.

Special Situation

DECEDENT WITH AN IRA or a QUALIFIED RETIREMENT PLAN ("QRP")

Anyone who is a beneficiary of an Individual Retirement Account ("IRA") or Qualified Retirement Plan ("QRP") needs to keep in mind is that, in general, no income taxes have been paid on monies placed such accounts. Once monies are withdrawn, significant taxes may be due. You need to learn what options are available to you as a beneficiary of the plan and the tax consequences of each option. You will need to ask an accountant how much will be due in taxes for each option. Once you know all the facts, you will be able to make the best choice for your circumstance.

SPOUSE

If the spouse is the beneficiary of the decedent's IRA account, then there are special options available. The spouse has the right to withdraw the money from the account or roll it over into the spouse's own retirement account. Although the employer can explain options that are available, the spouse still needs to understand the tax consequence of choosing any given option. It is important to consult with an accountant to determine the best way to go.

If the decedent had a QRP, the plan may permit the spouse to roll the balance of the account into a new IRA. The spouse needs to contact the decedent's employer for an explanation of the plan and all the options that are available at this time.

NOTIFYING IRS

THE FINAL INCOME TAX RETURN

The Personal Representative, or next of kin, needs to file the decedent's final federal and state income tax return. Filing the final return is done as part of filing the income tax return for the year of his death. If you have a joint bank account with the decedent, do not close that account until you determine whether the decedent is entitled to an income tax refund. See Chapter 6 for an explanation of how to obtain a refund from the IRS.

THE GOOD NEWS

Monies inherited from the decedent are generally not counted as income to you, so you do not pay federal income tax on those monies. If the monies you inherit later earn interest or income for you, then of course you will report that income as you do any other type of income.

Real and personal property inherited by a beneficiary is inherited at a "stepped up" basis. This means that if the decedent purchased some item that is now worth more than when he purchased it, then the beneficiary inherits the property at its fair market value as of the decedent's date of death. For example, suppose the decedent bought stock for $20,000 and it is now worth $50,000, then the beneficiary inherits the stock at the $50,000 value. If the beneficiary sells the stock for $50,000, he pays no tax. If the beneficiary holds onto the stock and later sells it for $60,000, the beneficiary will pay federal capital gains tax only on the $10,000 increase in value since the decedent's death.

SPOUSE

WIDOW'S HOMESTEAD TAX BENEFITS

If the decedent was receiving a homestead tax deduction because he was disabled or over 65, then the surviving spouse can receive those same tax deductions on the homestead, providing the surviving spouse is at lease 55 years of age. The surviving spouse needs to notify the municipal taxing collector of the death and apply for his/her own tax deduction (NJ 54:4-8.41a)

SELLING THE HOMESTEAD

In the tough "ole days" the IRS used to allow a once-in-a-lifetime, over age 55, up to $125,000 capital gains tax exclusion on the sale of the homestead (the principal residence). If a married couple sold their home and took the exclusion it was "used up" and no longer available to the other partner. In these, the good times, the IRS allows you to sell your homestead and up to $250,000 ($500,000 for a married couple) of the home-sale profit is tax free (IRC Section 121 B 3). There is no limit on the number of times you can use the exemption, provided you own and live in the homestead at least 2 years prior to the sale.

If the decedent and his spouse used their "once in a lifetime" homestead tax exemption, with this new law, the surviving spouse can sell the homestead and once again take advantage of a tax break.

FEDERAL AND STATE ESTATE TAXES

An ***Estate Tax*** is a tax imposed by the federal and state government for the transfer of property at death. The ***taxable estate*** of the decedent is the total value of all of his property, as of his date of death. This includes real property (homestead, vacant lots, etc.) and personal property (cars, life insurance policies, business interests, securities, IRA accounts, etc.). It includes property held in the decedent's name alone, as well as property that he held jointly or in trust for another.

The Federal government gives each person an Estate and Gift Tax Exclusion amount. No gift tax need be paid unless the decedent's taxable estate, plus gifts that he gave during his lifetime that exceeded $10,000 per person, per year, exceed the Exclusion amount. The Exclusion amount is scheduled to increase each year until the year 2006:

YEAR	EXCLUSION AMOUNT
2000 — 2001	$675,000
2002 — 2003	$700,000
2004	$850,000
2005	$950,000
2006	$1,000,000

No federal or state Estate Tax return need be filed unless the decedent's taxable estate and lifetime gifts exceed the scheduled amount as of his date of death. There is an unlimited marital tax deduction, so if the decedent was married, no estate tax need be paid; however if the decedent's estate exceeds the stated value, an estate tax return must be filed. If there is Federal Estate tax due, then the New Jersey Estate tax is equal to the federal estate tax credit, less the amount of state or federal inheritance or estate taxes actually paid to the state or federal government (NJ 54:38-1). The actual computation of the estate tax is complex. It is advisable to seek the counsel of an accountant or tax attorney to prepare both the state and federal return.

WHEN TO EVALUATE THE PROPERTY

When filing an estate tax return, the IRS gives you a choice of taking the value of the decedent's estate as of the date of death or 6 months later. The government's intent is to allow a reduction in estate taxes in the event that something happens during the 6 month period causing the property to lose its value. For example, suppose stock worth $500,000 is included as part of the decedent's estate. If the stock decreases to $400,000 within the 6 months following the death, then you can declare the $400,000 value. If the stock increases to $600,000, then you can still use the $500,000 date of death value.

The IRS does not allow the election unless the election will decrease the value of the gross estate and the total net estate taxes due. If there are little taxes due, then before deciding on a 6 month valuation date, you need to consider the cost of employing an accountant (or a tax attorney) to file the necessary tax forms. The cost in time and expense to make the election could be more than the tax payment itself. And also there is the more important consideration of the risk of holding onto the stock should the Bull market turn into a Bear. Paying less taxes may be small consolation for a sizeable loss in the value of the securities.

THE NEW JERSEY INHERITANCE TAX

The state of New Jersey has an inheritance tax. The amount of tax depends on the relationship of the beneficiary to the decedent. If the decedent's property is inherited by his spouse, parent, grandparent, child, or grandchildren, then there is no tax on the inheritance. There is no tax for property inherited by a brother, sister, daughter-in-law or son-in-law for transfers up to $25,000 in value; but anything over $25,000 (up to 1.1 million dollars) is taxed at a rate of 11%. Property inherited by anyone else is taxed at the rate of $15% for amounts up to $700,000 and 16% for amounts over $700,000 (NJ 54:33-1, 54:34-1, 54:34-2).

Any gift to an adopted child or a step-child is the same as to a natural child. Even a gift to a person who had a parent-child relationship with the decedent beginning before the child's 15th birthday and continued for 10 years is taxed as a gift to a child. Gifts to foster children might fall within this category (NJ 54:34-2.1).

A transfer of $500 or more made by the decedent within the 3 years prior to his death is subject to the inheritance tax unless the beneficiary of the gift can prove to the state tax commissioner that the decedent did not make the gift because the decedent knew he was about to die (NJ 54:34-1)

Certain deductions are allowed such as funeral expenses, the cost of the decedent's last illness, the cost of probate, certain debts owed by the decedent, taxes imposed by other states or the United States, etc. (NJ 54:34-5). If you have any question about the return you can call the New Jersey Division of Taxation at (609)292-5033; but as with the Estate Tax, it is best to have with an accountant or tax attorney assist with the preparation of the Inheritance Tax return.

GETTING TAX CLEARANCE

You have 9 months from the decedent's death to file the federal and New Jersey estate tax return. It is a good idea to consult with an accountant as soon as practicable after the death so you can make arrangements to pay any tax that may be due. If taxes are not timely paid then penalties may be due.

Still another reason to promptly attend to taxes, is that you may need tax clearance before you can get possession of many of the items owned by the decedent. For example, if the decedent had a stock certificate or a bank account in his name, the company will not transfer the property to the new owner without the written consent of the Director of the Division of Taxation. Transfers to the spouse, parent, child or grandchild of the decedent are exempt from this requirement because there is no inheritance tax for property they inherit (NJ 54:35-19).

You can get information about how to obtain a waiver or written consent from the New Jersey Division of Taxation by calling (609) 292-6400. You can also get information and download tax forms from their Web site:

NEW JERSEY DIVISION OF TAXATION
http://www.state.nj.us/treasury

Special Situation

DECEDENT WITH A TRUST

If the decedent was the Grantor (or Settlor) of a trust, then he was probably managing the trust as Trustee during his lifetime. The trust document should name a ***Successor Trustee*** to manage the trust now that the Grantor is deceased. The trust document may instruct the Successor Trustee to make certain gifts once the Grantor dies or the trust document may direct the Successor Trustee to hold money in trust for a beneficiary of the trust.

☎ LAWYER

IF YOU ARE SUCCESSOR TRUSTEE

If you are the Successor Trustee then in addition to following the terms of the trust, you are required to obey the laws of the state of New Jersey relating to the administration of the trust. For example, the law prohibits any self dealing or conflicts of interest. If the trust document allows trust funds to be used for your health, education, support or maintenance, then you cannot use those funds to pay off any of your personal obligations such as child support (NJ 3B:11-4.1). It is prudent to consult with an attorney experienced in Estate Planning to explain to you how to properly administer the trust to make sure that you do so without any liability to yourself.

IF YOU ARE A BENEFICIARY

If you are a beneficiary of the trust, then you need to obtain a copy of the trust and see how the trust is to be administered now that the Grantor or Settlor is deceased. Most trust documents are written in "legalese," so you may want to employ your own attorney to review the trust, and explain what rights you have under that trust.

NOTIFYING THE BUSINESS COMMUNITY

People and companies who were doing business with the decedent need to be notified of his death. This includes utility companies, credit card companies, banks, brokerage firms and any company that insured the decedent.

NOTIFY CREDIT CARD COMPANIES

You need to notify the decedent's credit card companies of the death. If you can find the contract with the credit card company check to see whether the decedent had credit card insurance. If the decedent had credit card insurance, then the balance of the account is now paid in full. If you cannot find the contract contact the company and get a copy of the contract along with a statement of the balance due as of the date of death.

DESTROY DECEDENT'S CREDIT CARDS

You need to destroy all of the decedent's credit cards. If you hold a credit card jointly with the decedent, then it is important to waste no time in closing that account and opening another in your name only.

That's something Barbara knows from hard experience. She and Hank were married for only a few months when Hank became ill with hepatitis. Hank came from a well to do family. They supported the couple during Hank's long illness. Hank put Barbara on all of his credit card accounts so that she could purchase things when he became too ill to go shopping with her.

After the funeral, Barbara had a gathering of friends and family at their apartment. Barbara was so preoccupied with her loss that she never noticed that Hank's credit cards were missing until the bills started coming in.

Barbara did not know who ran up the bills on Hank's credit cards during the month following his death. It was obvious that Hank's signature had been forged — but who forged it? One credit card company suspected that it might have been Barbara herself.

Because the cards were held jointly, it was Barbara's responsibility to straighten out the mess. Most of her credit card contracts required that she pay a fee of $50 for an unauthorized use of the card. She was able to clear her credit record but it took several weeks and hundreds of dollars to do so.

NOTIFY INSURANCE COMPANIES

Examine the decedent's financial records to determine the name and telephone number of all of the companies that insured the decedent or his property. This includes real property insurance, motor vehicle insurance, health insurance and life insurance.

MOTOR VEHICLE INSURANCE

If the decedent owned any type of motor vehicle (car, truck, boat, airplane) locate the insurance policy on that vehicle and notify the insurance company of the death. Determine how long insurance coverage continues after the death. Ask the insurance agent to explain what things are covered under the policy. Is the motor vehicle covered for all types of casualty (theft, accident, vandalism, etc.) or is coverage limited in some way?

If you can continue coverage then determine when the next insurance payment is due. Hopefully, the car will be sold or transferred to a beneficiary before that date, but if not, then you need to arrange to continue with insurance coverage.

Special Situation

ACCIDENTAL DEATH

If the decedent died as a result of an accident, then check for all possible sources of accident insurance coverage including his homeowner's policy. Some credit card companies provide accident insurance as part of their contract with their card holders.

If the decedent died in an automobile accident, check to see whether he was covered by any type of travel insurance, such as rental car insurance. If he belonged to an automobile club, such as AAA, then check whether he had accident insurance as part of his club membership.

LIFE INSURANCE COMPANIES

If the decedent had life insurance, then you need to locate the policy and notify the company of his death. Call each life insurance company and ask what they require in order to forward the insurance proceeds to the beneficiary. Most companies will ask you to send them the original policy and a certified copy of the death certificate.

Send the original policy by certified mail or any of the overnight services that require a signed receipt for the package. Make a copy of the original policy for your records before mailing the original policy to the company.

IF YOU CANNOT LOCATE THE POLICY

If you know that the decedent was insured but you cannot locate the insurance policy, the AMERICAN COUNCIL OF LIFE INSURANCE ("ACLI") may be able to help you. Write to the ACLI giving them the name, address, date of birth, and social security number of the decedent. Their address is:

POLICY SEARCH ACLI
1000 Pennsylvania Avenue, NW
Washington, DC 20004

The ACLI will assist you by asking the 100 largest insurance companies in the nation to search their records for the missing policy. If it is found, you will receive a copy of the policy free of charge.

IF YOU CANNOT LOCATE THE COMPANY

If you cannot locate the insurance company it may be doing business under another name or it may no longer be doing business in the state of New Jersey. Each state has a branch of government that regulates insurance companies doing business in that state. If you are having difficulty locating the insurance company call the Department of Insurance in the state where the policy was purchased and ask for assistance in locating the company. The number for the New Jersey Insurance Department is (609) 292-4337.

EAGLE PUBLISHING COMPANY OF BOCA has the telephone number for the Department of Insurance for each state at their Web site:

EAGLE PUBLISHING COMPANY OF BOCA WEB SITE
http://www.eaglepublishing.com

WORK RELATED INSURANCE

If the decedent was employed then his employer may provide survivor benefits from a company or group life insurance plan and/or a retirement plan. If the decedent belonged to a union, then check with the union to determine whether members of the union receive any death benefits.

The decedent may have belonged to a professional, fraternal or social organization such as the local Chamber of Commerce, a Veteran's organization, the Kiwanis, AARP, the Rotary Club, etc. If he belonged to any such organization check to see whether the organization provided any type of insurance coverage.

Special Situation

BUSINESS OWNED BY DECEDENT

If the decedent owned his own company he may have purchased "key man" insurance. Key man insurance is a policy designed to protect the company should a valuable employee become disabled or die. Benefits are paid to the company to compensate the company for the loss of someone who is essential to the continuation of the business. Ultimately the policy benefits those who inherit the business.

If the decedent owned shares in the company or was a partner in the company, there may be a shareholder's agreement or partnership agreement requiring the company to use the insurance proceeds to purchase the shares or partnership interest owned by the decedent. If there is a probate procedure, then the Personal Representative's attorney will need to review the agreement. If no probate is necessary, then the next of kin need to find out what rights (if any) the family has in the business or to the proceeds of the key man insurance policy.

Special Situation

CORPORATE OWNER OR REGISTERED AGENT

If the decedent was the sole owner a corporation, then there may need to be a probate procedure in order to transfer the company to the new owner. If the decedent was the sole officer and Registered Agent of the company, then the North Jersey Corporations Division needs to be notified of the identity of the new officers and Registered Agent.

The law requires each corporation to continuously maintain a Registered Agent who resides in this state. If the decedent was the Resident Agent of a corporation, then a new person must be appointed as soon as is practicable (NJ 14A:4-1, 14A:4-3).

Forms to change officers, directors and Registered Agents can be obtained by calling the New Jersey Division of Administration (609) 292-9862 or by writing to: New Jersey - Division of Administration
P.O. Box 459
Trenton, NJ 08625

If you were not actively involved in running the business, then you might request a status report of the company. The report will show whether filing fees are current and will identify the officers and directors of the company. New Jersey has a Web site from which you can download forms and obtain information about New Jersey corporations.

NJ CORPORATION INFORMATION WEB SITE
http://accessnet.state.nj.us/Browse.asp

If the decedent owned his own home, then check whether there is sufficient insurance coverage on the property. The decedent may have neglected to increase his insurance as the property appreciated in value. If you think the property may be vacant for some period of time, then it is important to have vandalism coverage included in the policy. Once the property is sold, or transferred to the proper beneficiary, you can have the policy discontinued or transferred to the new owner. The decedent's estate should receive a rebate for the unused portion of the premium.

NOTIFY THE HOMEOWNER'S ASSOCIATION

If the decedent owned a condominium or a residence regulated by a homeowner's association, then the association needs to be notified of the death. Once the property is transferred to the proper beneficiary, he/she will need to contact the association and arrange to have notices of dues or assessments forwarded to the new owner.

MORTGAGE INSURANCE

If the decedent had a mortgage on any parcel of real estate that he owned, he might have arranged with his lender for an insurance policy that pays off the mortgage balance in the event of his death. Look at the closing statement to see if there was a charge for mortgage insurance. Also, check with the lender to determine if such a policy was purchased.

If the decedent was the sole owner of the property, then the beneficiary of that property needs to make arrangements to continue payment of the mortgage until title to the property is transferred to that beneficiary.

HEALTH INSURANCE

The Health Insurance carrier probably knows of the death, but it is a good idea to contact them to determine what coverage the decedent had under that insurance plan. If you cannot find the original policy, have the insurance company send you a copy of the policy so that you can determine whether medical treatment given to the decedent before his death was covered by that policy

Special Situation

DECEDENT ON MEDICARE

If the decedent was covered by Medicare, you do not need to notify anyone, but you do need to know what things were covered by Medicare so that you can determine what medical bills are (or are not) covered by Medicare. The publication MEDICARE AND YOU explains what things are covered. The book is available in regular print (Publication HCFA 10050) and in large print (Publication HCFA 10050-LE). You can get the book by writing to the

U.S. GOVERNMENT PRINTING OFFICE
U.S. Dept. of Health and Human Services
Health Care Financing Administration
7500 Security Boulevard
Baltimore, MD 21244-1850

The publication is also available on the Internet:

MEDICARE WEB SITE
http:/www.medicare.gov

SPOUSE

THE SPOUSE'S HEALTH INSURANCE

If the spouse of the decedent is insured under Medicare, then the death does not affect the surviving spouse's coverage. If spouse was not covered by Medicare but has her own health insurance that also covered the decedent, then the spouse needs to notify the employer of the death because this may affect the cost of the plan to the employer and/or the spouse.

If the spouse was covered under the decedent's policy then he/she needs to arrange for new coverage. There are state and federal laws that ensure continued coverage under the decedent's policy for a period of time depending on whether the decedent's employer falls under federal or state regulation.

If the decedent was employed by a federally regulated company (usually a company with at least twenty employees) then under the Consolidated Omnibus Budget Reconciliation Act ("COBRA") the employer must make the company health plan available to the surviving spouse and any dependent child of the decedent for at least 36 months. The employer is required to give notice to the surviving spouse that the spouse and/or dependent child have the right to continue coverage under the decedent's health plan. The spouse and/or child have 60 days from the date of death or 60 days after the employer sends notice (whichever is later) to tell the employer whether the surviving spouse and child wish to continue with the health insurance plan (29 USC 18 Sec. 1162, 1163).

SPOUSE'S HEALTH INSURANCE (continued)

The only problem with continued coverage may be the cost. Before the death, the employer may have been paying some percentage of the premium. The employer has no such duty after the death unless there was some employment agreement stating otherwise. Under COBRA, the employer may charge the spouse for the full cost of the plan plus a 2% administrative fee. If you have a question about your coverage under COBRA, you can call the U.S. Department of Labor ("DOL") at (800) 998-7542 and ask for the number of your local DOL office. You can also ask that they send you their publication HEALTH BENEFITS UNDER COBRA; or you can visit their Web site for more information:

DEPARTMENT OF LABOR WEB SITE

http://www.dol.gov/dol/pwba

CONTINUED COVERAGE UNDER NEW JERSEY LAW

If the decedent's employer is not regulated under COBRA, then company's insurance coverage may be regulated under New Jersey law. The New Jersey law regulating health insurance is similar to COBRA, but with different time constraints. Coverage need only continue for 12 months and the spouse and/or dependent child has just 30 days from the date of death to let the employer know that they wish to continue with the coverage. Again, cost may be a problem. As with COBRA, the spouse can be charged the full cost of the policy plus an additional 2%. The spouse may find it less costly to seek health insurance elsewhere (NJ 17B:27A-27).

NOTIFY ADVERTISERS

Probably the last in the world to learn of the decedent's death is the direct mail advertiser. Advertisers are nothing if not tenacious. It is not uncommon for advertisements to be mailed to the decedent for more than ten years after the death. It is not because the advertiser is trying to sell something to the decedent, but rather the people who prepare (and sell) mailing lists do not know that the person is dead.

Those who sell mailing lists may not be motivated to update the list because of the cost of doing the necessary research; and perhaps because the price of the mailing list is often based on the number of people on the list. Even those who compose their own list may decide it is less costly to mail to everyone, than take the time (and money) to update the list.

If it gives you pleasure to think of advertisers spending substantial sums for nothing, then that is what you should do (nothing). But for those of you who wince each time you see another piece of mail addressed to the decedent, you can write to the Direct Marketing Association and ask that his name be deleted from all mailing lists:

Mail Preference Service
Direct Marketing Association
P.O. Box 9008
Farmingdale, NY 11735

You will need to give them the decedent's complete address, including zip code and every name variation that the decedent may have used; for example:

Mr. Theodore James Jones
Ted Jones   Ted J. Jones
T. J. Jones   T. James Jones, etc.

✍ CHANGE BENEFICIARIES ✍

If the decedent was someone you named as beneficiary of your insurance policy, Will or trust, brokerage account or pension plan, then you may need to name another beneficiary in his place:

INSURANCE POLICY ✍

If you named the decedent as the primary beneficiary of your life insurance policy, then check to see whether you named a contingent (alternate) beneficiary in the event that the decedent did not survive you. If not, then you need to contact the insurance company and name a new beneficiary. If you did name a contingent beneficiary, then that person is now your primary beneficiary and you need to consider whether you wish to name a new contingent beneficiary at this time.

HEALTH INSURANCE POLICY ✍

If the decedent was covered under your health insurance policy, then your employer and the health insurer need to be notified of the death because this may affect the cost of the plan to you and/or your employer.

WILL OR TRUST ✍

Most Wills provide for a contingent beneficiary in the event that the person named as beneficiary dies first. If you named the decedent as your beneficiary, then check to see whether you named an alternate beneficiary. If not, you need to have your attorney revise your Will and name a new beneficiary.

Similarly, if you are the Grantor or Settlor of a trust and the decedent was one of the beneficiaries of your trust, then check the trust document to see if you named an alternate beneficiary. If not, contact your attorney to prepare an amendment to the trust, naming a new beneficiary.

BANK AND SECURITIES ACCOUNTS ✍

If the decedent was a beneficiary of your bank or securities account, or if the decedent was a joint owner of your bank account or securities account, then it is important to contact the financial institution and tell them about the death. You may wish to arrange for a new beneficiary or joint owner at this time.

PENSION PLANS ✍

If the decedent was a beneficiary under your pension plan, then you need to notify them of his death and name a new beneficiary. Many pension plans require that you notify them within a set period of time (usually 30 days) so it is important to notify them as soon as you are able. If the decedent was a beneficiary of your Individual Retirement Account ("IRA") or of your Qualified Retirement Plan ("QRP") and you did not provide for an alternate beneficiary, then you need to name someone at this time.

There are many government regulations relating to IRA and QRP accounts. For example, you must begin to withdraw money from the account on April 1st of the year after you reach the age of 70 1/2. How much you must withdraw depends on whether you choose to base the amount withdrawn on your own life expectancy or on the joint life expectancy of you and your oldest beneficiary. If you have not reached the age of 70 1/2, then before naming a new beneficiary, you may wish to consult with your accountant to decide which is the best option for you.

NOTIFYING CREDITORS

If a probate procedure is necessary and the decedent owed money, then it is the job of the person appointed as Personal Representative to notify the decedent's creditors of the death. The attorney who handles the probate will explain to the Personal Representative how notice is to be given.

If no probate procedure is necessary, then the next of kin can notify the creditors of the death, but before doing so, read Chapter 4: WHAT BILLS NEED TO BE PAID? That chapter explains what bills need to be paid and who is responsible to pay them.

Before any bill can be paid you need to know whether the decedent left any assets that could be used to pay those debts. The next chapter explains how to identify, and then locate all of the property owned by the decedent.

Locating the Assets 3

It is important to locate the financial records of the decedent and then carefully examine those records. Even the partner of a long-term marriage should conduct a thorough search because the surviving spouse may be unaware of all that was owned (or owed) by the decedent.

It is not unusual for a surviving spouse to be surprised when learning of the decedent's business transactions — especially in those cases where the decedent had control of family finances. One such example is that of Sam and Helen. They married just as soon as Sam was discharged from the army after World War II. During their marriage, Sam handled all of the finances, giving Helen just enough money to run the household.

Every now and again Helen would think of getting a job. She longed to have her own source of income and some economic independence. Each time she brought up the subject Sam would loudly object. He had no patience for this new "woman's lib" thing. Sam said he got married to have a real wife — one who would cook his meals and keep house for him.

Helen was not the arguing type. She rationalized, saying that Sam had a delicate stomach and dust allergies. He needed her to prepare his special meals and keep an immaculate house for him. Besides, Sam had a good job with a major cruise line and he needed her to accompany him on his frequent business trips.

Once Sam retired, he was even more cautious in his spending habits. Helen seldom complained. She assumed the reason for his "thrift" was that they had little money and had to live on his pension.

They were married 52 years when Sam died at the age of 83. Helen was 81 at the time of his death. She was one very happy, very angry and very aged widow when she discovered that Sam left her with assets worth well over a million dollars!

LOCATING FINANCIAL RECORDS

To locate the decedent's assets you need to find evidence of what he owned and where those assets are located. His financial records should lead you to the location of all of his assets so your first job is to locate those records. The best place to start the search is in the decedent's home. Many people keep their financial records in a single place but it is important to check the entire house to be sure you did not miss something.

CHECK THE COMPUTER

Don't overlook that computer sitting silently in the corner. It may hold the decedent's check register and all of the decedent's financial records. The computer may be programmed to protect information. If you cannot access the decedent's records, you may need to employ a computer technician or computer consultant who will be able to print out all of the information on the hard drive of the computer. You can find such a technician or consultant by looking in the telephone book under

COMPUTER SUPPORT SERVICES or
COMPUTER SYSTEM DESIGNS & CONSULTANTS.

COLLECT AND IDENTIFY KEYS

The decedent may have kept his records in a safe deposit box, so you may find that your first job is to locate the keys to the box. As you go through the personal effects of the decedent, collect and identify all the keys that you find. If you come across an unidentified key, it could be a key to a post office box (private or federal) or a safe deposit box located in a bank or in a private vault company. You will need to determine whether that key opens a box that contains property belonging to the decedent or whether the key is to a box no longer in use. Some ways to investigate are as follows:

☑ CHECK BUSINESS RECORDS

If the decedent kept receipts, look through those items to see if he paid for the rental of a post office or safe deposit box. Also, check his check register to see if he wrote out a check to the Postmaster or to any safe deposit or vault company. Look at his bank statements to see if there is any bank charge for a safe deposit box. Some banks bill separately for safe deposit boxes so check with all of the banks in which the decedent had an account to determine if he had a box with that bank.

☑ CHECK THE KEY TYPE

If you cannot identify the key take the key to all of the local locksmiths and ask whether anyone can identify the type of facility that uses such keys. If that doesn't work then go to each bank, post office and private safe deposit boxes located in places where the decedent shopped, worked or frequented and ask whether they use the type of key that you found.

☑ CHECK THE MAIL

Check the mail over the next several months to see if the decedent receives a statement requesting payment for the next year's rental of a post office or safe deposit box.

You may find evidence of a brokerage account, bank account, or safe deposit box by examining correspondence addressed to the decedent. If the decedent was living alone, then have the mail forwarded to the person he named as Personal Representative or Executor of his Will. If the decedent did not leave a Will then the mail should be forwarded to his next of kin. Call the Postmaster and ask him/her to send you the necessary forms to make the change. Request that the mail be forwarded for the longest period allowed by law (currently one year).

The decedent may have been renting a post office box at his local post office branch or perhaps at the branch closest to where he did his banking. Ask the Postmaster to help you determine whether the decedent was renting a post office box. If so, then you need to locate the key to the box so that you can collect the decedent's mail.

Special Situation LOST POST OFFICE BOX KEY

If the decedent had a post office box and you cannot locate the key, then contact the local postmaster and ask him/her what documentation is needed for you to gain possession of the mail in that box. As before, you will ask the Postmaster to have all future mail addressed to that box, forwarded to the Personal Representative, or if there is no Will, then to the decedent's next of kin.

WHAT TO DO WITH CHECKS

You may receive checks in the mail made out to the decedent. Social security checks, pension checks and annuity checks issued after the date of death need to be returned to the sender (see pages 28 and 30). Other checks need to be deposited to the decedent's bank account. The decedent is not here to endorse the check, but you can deposit to his account by writing his bank account number on the back of the check and printing beneath it "FOR DEPOSIT ONLY." The bank will accept such an endorsement and deposit the check into the decedent's account. If the check is significant in value and/or the decedent had different accounts that are accessible to different people, then there needs to be cooperation and a sense of fair play. If not, the dollar gain may not nearly offset the emotional turmoil. Such was the case with Gail.

Gail's father made her a joint owner of his checking account to assist in paying his bills. He had macular degeneration and it was increasingly difficult for him to see. The father also had a savings account that was in his name only.

Gail's brother, Richard, had a good paying job in Miami. Even though he lived at a distance, Richard, his wife and two children always spent the spring school break holidays with his father. Gail's good cooking added to the festivities.

Winters were still another time for a visit with Richard and his family. Their father enjoyed leaving the raw New Jersey winter to spend a few weeks with Richard in the warm Florida sunshine. Just before New Years, the father purchased a round trip ticket to Miami. It cost several hundred dollars. Before the departure date, the father had a heart attack and died.

Gail called the airline to cancel the ticket. They refunded the money in a check made out to her father. She deposited the check into the joint account.

As part of the probate procedure, the money in the father's savings account was divided equally between Richard and his sister. Richard wondered what happened to the money from the airline tickets. Gail explained "He paid for the tickets from the joint account, so I deposited the money back to the joint account. "

"Aren't you going to give me half?"

"Dad meant for me to have whatever was in that joint account. If he wanted you to have half of the money, he would have made you joint owner as well."

Richard didn't see it that way:
"That refund was part of Dad's probate estate. It should have been deposited to his savings account to be divided equally between us. Are you going force me to argue this in court?"

Gail finally agreed to split the money with Richard, but the damage was done.

Gail complains that holidays are lonely since her father died.

LOCATE OUT OF STATE ACCOUNTS

If the decedent had out of state bank or brokerage accounts, then you might be able to locate them if they mail the decedent monthly or quarterly statements. Not all institutions do so, but all institutions are required to send out an IRS tax form 1099 each year giving the amount of interest earned on that account. Once those forms come in, you will learn the location of all of the decedent's active accounts.

COLLECT LEGAL DOCUMENTS

As you go through the papers of the decedent you may come across documents that indicate property ownership, such as bank registers, title to motor vehicles, stock or bond certificates, insurance policies, brokerage account statements, etc. Place all evidence of ownership in a single place. You will need to contact different institutions to transfer title to the proper beneficiary. Chapter 5 explains how to identify the proper beneficiary. Chapter 6 explains how to transfer the property to that beneficiary.

LOCATING TITLE TO THE MOTOR VEHICLE

In the state of New Jersey, if monies are owed on a car, then the lender takes possession of the certificate of title until the loan is paid. If you cannot find the original certificate of title, then it is either lost or monies are owed on the car and the lienholder has the title. To get information and obtain a copy of the title you can go to the local Motor Vehicle Services office. You can save time if you first call to determine what information they require. The in-state toll free number is (888) 486-3339. If you are calling from out-of-state, then call (609) 292-6500.

If you find there is a lien on the car then contact the lienholder and get a copy of the contract that is the basis of the loan. You may find that the car is leased and not owned by the decedent. If so, contact the lessor and get a copy of the lease agreement. Once you have the contract, check to see whether the decedent had life insurance as part of the agreement. If he did, then the lease is now paid in full. The next of kin or the Personal Representative can send the death certificate to the leasing company with a copy of the contract and a letter requesting that the paid contract be transferred to the beneficiary who can use the car for the remainder of the leasing period, or take title to the car, whichever option is available under the lease agreement.

COLLECT DEEDS

Collect the deeds to all property owned by the decedent. Many people keep deeds in a safe deposit box. If you cannot find the deed in the decedent's home, then you need to determine whether he had a safe deposit box. (See the end of this Chapter for information about how to get into the safe deposit box.)

If you know that the decedent owned real property (lot, residence, condominium, cooperative, time share, etc.) but you cannot locate the deed, then contact the county recorder, in the county in which the property is located, and ask for a copy of the deed. You will need to identify the parcel of land by giving the legal description of the land or its parcel identification number. You can find this information on the last tax bill sent to the decedent. If you cannot find the last tax bill, then call the Treasurer or County Collector or Assessor for the information.

You can use the same procedure if you cannot locate the deed to property owned by the decedent in another state, namely, check with the recording department in the county where the property is located. Many states keep their land records in the court house. You can call the Clerk of the Circuit Court for information. In other states there is a separate recording department and you may need to contact the County Recorder or Register of Deeds.

Special Situation

RESIDENTIAL LEASE

If the decedent was renting his residence, then he may have a written lease agreement. It is important to locate the lease because the decedent's estate may be responsible for payments under the lease. If you cannot locate the lease, then ask the landlord for a copy. If the landlord reports that there was no written lease, then verify that the decedent was on a month to month basis and then work out a mutually agreeable time in which to vacate the premises.

If a written lease is in effect, then determine the end of the lease period, and whether there was a security deposit. Ask whether the landlord will agree to cancel the lease on the condition that the property is left in good condition. If the landlord says that the estate is responsible to pay the balance of the lease, then it is prudent to have an attorney review the lease to determine what rights and responsibilities remain now that the tenant is deceased.

☎ LAWYER

ONGOING BUSINESS

If the decedent was the sole owner of a business, or if he owned a partnership interest in a business, the Personal Representative needs to contact the company accountant to obtain the company's business records. If there is a company attorney, then the attorney may be able to assist in obtaining the records. If you are a beneficiary of the estate, consider consulting with your own attorney to determine what rights and responsibilities you may have in the business.

COLLECT TAX RECORDS

You will need to file the decedent's final state and federal income tax return so you need to collect all of his tax records that he filed for the past 3 years. If you cannot locate his prior tax records, then check his personal telephone book and/or his personal bank register to see if he employed an accountant. If you can locate his accountant, then contact the accountant to see if he/she has a copy of those records.

If you are unable to locate the decedent's federal tax records then they can be obtained from the IRS. The IRS will send copies of the decedent's tax filings to anyone who has a ***fiduciary relationship*** with the decedent. The IRS considers the following people to be fiduciaries:

- The person named as Personal Representative (or Executor) of the decedent's Will
- The Successor Trustee of the decedent's trust
- If the person died without a Will, then whoever is legally entitled to possession of the decedent's property.

See Chapter 5 to determine who are the beneficiaries.

To notify the IRS of the fiduciary capacity, you need to file Form 56: NOTICE CONCERNING FIDUCIARY RELATIONSHIP

To request the copies, file IRS Form 4506:
REQUEST FOR COPY OR TRANSCRIPT OF TAX FORM
Your accountant can file these forms for you or you can obtain the forms from the IRS by calling (800) 829-3676 or you can download them from the Internet:

IRS FORMS WEB SITE
http://www.irs.gov/forms_pubs/forms.html

STATE INCOME TAX RETURN

If you cannot locate the decedent's state income tax return you can obtain copies from the New Jersey Division of Taxation. The procedure for obtaining a copy is much the same as that of the IRS. The Division of Taxation will provide a copy of the decedent's return to anyone in a fiduciary relationship to the decedent. If the copy of the return is being requested by someone other that the decedent's spouse, the Division may require that a Personal Representative be appointed by the probate court before they will forward a copy of the decedent's tax records.

You can call the New Jersey Division of Taxation at (609) 292-1359 and ask what information they require in order to obtain a copy of the decedent's tax returns or you can write to: The Office of the State Treasurer
The New Jersey Division of Taxation
P.O. Box 002
Trenton, NJ 08625

If the decedent was forgetful, he may have money in a lost bank or securities account or abandoned safe deposit box. New Jersey law requires that if the owner of the property has not claimed it for period of time and the owner of the property cannot be found after a diligent search, then the property must be turned over to the New Jersey Department of the Treasury. Most items are declared abandoned after 5 years; for example, an uncashed check is considered unclaimed after 5 years; but the time period can vary for specific items, such as:

- 1 year for a utility deposit after service is discontinued
- 7 years for an uncashed money order
- 15 years for an uncashed traveler's check

(NJ 46:30B-7, 46:30B-11, 46:30B-12, 46:30B-16, 46:30B-29)

The Treasury Department will hold an abandoned security for one year, and then sell it at the current market value. The Department will sell, at auction, tangible items, such as jewelry within three years of receiving the item. Anyone who later makes a valid claim for the property will receive the net proceeds of the sale (NJ 46:30B-69, 46:30B-71, 46:30B-79).

You can determine whether there is a record identifying the decedent as the owner of abandoned property by completing the Unclaimed Property Form. You can get the form from the Unclaimed Property Administration at (609) 292-8822 or by writing to:

STATE OF NEW JERSEY, UNCLAIMED PROPERTY
ATTN: Claims Section
P.O. Box 214
Trenton, NJ 08685-0214

The New Jersey Treasury Department has a Web site that lists the name of owners of unclaimed property. You can download the Unclaimed Property Form from that Web site.

NJ UNCLAIMED PROPERTY WEB SITE
http:// www.state.nj.us/treasury/taxation

CLAIMS FOR DECEDENT VICTIM OF HOLOCAUST

The New York State Banking Department has a special Claims Processing Office for Holocaust survivors or their heirs. The office processes claims for Swiss bank accounts that were dormant since the end of World War II. If the decedent was a victim of the Holocaust, you can get information about money that may be due to the decedent's estate by calling (800) 695-3318.

CLAIMS IN OTHER STATES

Each state has an agency or department that is responsible for handling lost, abandoned or unclaimed property located within that state. If the decedent had residences in other states, then call the UNCLAIMED or ABANDONED PROPERTY department to see if the decedent has unclaimed property in that state.

EAGLE PUBLISHING COMPANY OF BOCA lists telephone numbers for the unclaimed property division for each state at their Web site:

EAGLE PUBLISHING COMPANY OF BOCA WEB SITE
http://www.eaglepublishing.com

LOCATE CONTRACTS

If the decedent belonged to a health club or gym, he may have prepaid for the year. Look for the club contract. It will give the terms of the agreement. If you cannot locate the contract then contact the company for a copy of the agreement. If the contract was prepaid, then determine whether the agreement provides for a refund for the unused portion.

SERVICE CONTRACT

Many people purchase appliance service contracts to have their appliances serviced in the event that an appliance should need repair. If the decedent had a security system then he may have had a service contract with a company to monitor the system and contact the police in the event of a break-in.

If the decedent had a service contract, then you need to locate it and determine whether it can be assigned to the new owner of the property. If the contract is assignable, the new owner can reimburse the decedent's estate for the unused portion. If the contract cannot be assigned, then once the property is transferred, try to obtain a refund for the unused portion of the contract.

LOCATE OUT OF STATE ACCOUNTS

If the decedent had out of state bank or brokerage accounts, then you might be able to locate them if they mail the decedent monthly or quarterly statements. Not all institutions do so, but all institutions are required to send out an IRS tax form 1099 each year giving the amount of interest earned on that account. Once those forms come in, you will learn the location of all of the decedent's active accounts.

LOCATING THE WILL

New Jersey law requires that the decedent's Will cannot be admitted to probate until at least 10 days have passed from his date of death. The person who has the decedent's original Will must file it with the Surrogate in the county where decedent resided (NJ 3B:3-22). There is only one original Will, so it is important to hand carry the original document to the Surrogate.

Each county has a different probate procedure. Some Surrogates require an appointment. Others allow walk-ins. You may save yourself time if you first call the Surrogate and determine what is required in that county. It is important to make a copy of the Will for your own records before delivering it to the Surrogate.

☎ **LAWYER**

OUT OF STATE RESIDENCE

If the decedent owned property in New Jersey, but had his primary residence in another state, then before delivering the Will to the Surrogate, you need to determine the best place to begin the probate procedure. Convenience and the cost of probate are important, but you also should consider that each state has its own tax structure. It is a good idea to consult with a probate attorney in the state of his residence as well as one in New Jersey. Ask each attorney whether the location of the probate procedure will have any effect on who is to inherit the property or how much the estate will be taxed. If there is a Will and it would be to your advantage to have it probated in New Jersey, then that Will can be admitted to probate in New Jersey (NJ 3B:3-28).

☎ LAWYER

OUT OF STATE PROPERTY

If the decedent had his residence in New Jersey but he had property in another state, then under New Jersey law if he died without a Will, if it is necessary to conduct a probate procedure, then it must be done in New Jersey (NJ 3B:10-13). Whoever wishes to apply for Letters must do so in the Surrogates' Court in the county where the decedent lived. Once Letters are issued, the Personal Representative will need to arrange to transfer the property in the other state. He will need to contact an attorney who is experienced in Probate matters in the other state to determine whether a an ***ancillary*** (secondary) probate procedure needs to be conducted in that state.

If the decedent left a Will, then consult with your attorney to determine whether to Probate the Will in this state or the state where his property is located.

Special Situation

WILL DRAFTED IN ANOTHER STATE OR COUNTRY

The state of New Jersey respects the laws of other states and countries. If a Will is drafted in another state or country and executed according to the laws of that state or country, then it is valid in the state of New Jersey (NJ 3B:3-9).

If the Will is written in a foreign language, then it must be accompanied by a true and complete English translation before it can be admitted to Probate.

THE MISSING WILL

Most people put off making a Will until they think they need to. For most people that need arises when they are elderly and/or seriously ill and have assets that they want to leave to someone. If the decedent was relatively young, with few assets, and you cannot find a Will, then he probably died without one.

Those who make a Will, usually tell the person that they appoint as Executor, of the existence of the Will. Chances are, that someone in the decedent's circle of family and friends, knows whether or not there is a Will. If you don't come across a Will, then check to see if the decedent told anyone about having a Will. If you believe that the decedent had a Will, but you cannot find it, then there are at least three places to check out:

⇨ THE SURROGATE

Anyone who has possession of the Will can deposit it with the Surrogate in the county of the decedent's residence. You may want to check with the Surrogate to see if it the Will has been deposited with the court.

⇨ THE SAFE DEPOSIT BOX

If you believe that the decedent had a Will but you cannot find it, then check to see whether the decedent had a safe deposit box. If he did, you will need to gain entry to that box to see whether the Will is in the box. See page 73 for an explanation of how to gain entry to the safe deposit box.

➪ THE DECEDENT'S ATTORNEY

Look at the decedent's checkbook for the past few years and see whether he paid any attorney fees. If you are able to locate the decedent's attorney, then call and inquire whether the attorney ever drafted a Will for the decedent, and if so, whether the attorney has the original Will in his possession. If the attorney has the original Will, then ask the attorney to file the Will with the Surrogate. Asking the attorney to forward the Will to the court does not obligate you to employ the attorney should you later find that a probate procedure is necessary.

☎ LAWYER **A COPY AND NO ORIGINAL**

If you have a copy of the Will but cannot locate the original then the court will allow the estate of the decedent to be probated using the copy, provided you can prove that the document is a true copy of the decedent's valid, unrevoked Will (NJ 3B:3-19). You will need to employ an attorney who is experienced in probate matters to present such proof to the court.

ACCESSING THE SAFE DEPOSIT BOX

Accessibility to a safe deposit box is governed by the agreement signed by the decedent when he rented the box. If the decedent rented the box jointly with his spouse (or family member), each with authority to enter the box, then that person can access the box. If the decedent rented the box in his name only, and his agreement with the Lessor (usually a bank) gave someone (an Agent) authority to enter the box, then that authority continues until the the Lessor is notified of the death. Once the lessor learns of the death, they will not allow access to the box until a Personal Representative is appointed and has authority to take possession of the decedent's assets (NJ 17:14A-52, 46:39-4).

If the decedent was the only person with access to the safe deposit box and you believe there may be a Will in the box, you can call the bank and ask the bank officer to examine the contents of the box. If the Will is in the box, then you can ask the bank to forward the Will to the Surrogate's Court.

What Bills Need To Be Paid? 4

It is the Personal Representative's job to determine whether the decedent owed any money, and if so, then to give each creditor an opportunity to present their ***claim*** (demand for payment) against the estate. If the decedent had many debts, there may not be enough money in the estate to pay all of the bills. The only remaining question is whether anyone else might be responsible to pay those bills. If the decedent was married, then the first person the creditor will look to is the decedent's spouse. To understand the basis of this obligation you need to know a bit of our legal history.

We inherited our legal system from England. Under the old English common law, once a woman married, her legal identity merged with that of her husband. A married woman had no right to own property or to enter into a contract in her own name. Once married, a woman became totally dependent on her husband and he was legally responsible to provide her with basic necessities including medical services. If anyone provided these necessities to his wife, then regardless of whether the husband agreed to be responsible for the debt, he was obliged to pay for them. This law was called the DOCTRINE OF NECESSARIES.

Here in the United States a series of Married Women's Rights Acts were passed giving married women the right to own property and to enter into a contract without her husband's permission. After Married Women's Rights laws were passed, a series of cases arose in many states that tested whether the Doctrine of Necessaries still applied in that state. Questions that judges had to decide were:

> *If a wife can own property and contract to pay for her own necessaries, should her husband be responsible for these debts, in the event that she does not have enough money to pay for them?*
>
> *And if the husband is responsible for his wife's debts, should she be responsible for his?*

In New Jersey the answer was "yes" to both questions (*Jersey Shore Medical Center-Fitkin Hospital v. Estate of Baum,* 417 A.2d 1003, 1010 (1980)). Anyone who provides necessaries for a married person in this state has the right to demand payment from the spouse — whether or not the supporting partner agreed to be personally liable to pay for those necessaries.

This right continues after death. If the decedent was married and owed money for necessaries then the creditor can demand payment from the decedent's estate. If there are not sufficient funds in the estate, then the creditor can look to the spouse to pay the debt.

In this chapter we discuss the responsibilities of the surviving spouse, as well as others who may be responsible to pay debts left by the decedent, beginning with joint debts.

JOINT DEBTS

A ***joint debt*** is a debt that two or more people are responsible to pay. Usually the contract or promissory note reads that both parties agree to ***joint and several*** liability, meaning they both agree to pay the debt and each of them, individually, agree to be pay the debt. A joint debt can also be in the form of monies owed by one person with payment guaranteed by another person. If the person who owes the money does not pay, then the ***guarantor*** is responsible to pay the debt.

Before paying a bill, determine whether it is the decedent's debt or a joint debt. Hospital bills, nursing home bills, funeral expenses, legal fees incurred because of the decedent's death are all debts of the decedent's estate. They are not joint debts unless someone guaranteed payment for the monies owed.

PAYING FOR THE JOINT DEBT

If another person is jointly responsible for monies owed by the decedent, then that bill should be paid from any joint account held with the decedent. If the joint debtor did not have a joint account with the decedent, then the joint debtor must pay the bill from his/her own funds.

SPOUSE

DEBTS THE SPOUSE MUST PAY

The surviving spouse may need to pay for the decedent's necessaries, but not for any other debt unless the debt was joint (NJ 37: 2-10). Loans signed by the decedent and his spouse are joint debts, as are charges on credit cards that both were authorized to use. Property taxes are a joint debt if the decedent and the spouse both owned the property.

JOINT PROPERTY BUT NO JOINT DEBT

Suppose all of the decedent's funds are held jointly with a family member and the family member did not agree to pay any of the decedent's debts? Can a creditor require that the decedent's share of the joint funds be set aside to pay the debt?

The answer to this question depends on how the property is titled. If the property is held ***jointly*** or ***jointly with rights of survivorship***, then the surviving owner owns the property as of the date of death. There is no right of survivorship if the property is owned by the decedent and another as ***tenants in common***. The decedent's creditor has the right to demand that the decedent's share of such property be used to pay the debt. This applies to bank accounts, securities, or real property that the decedent owned as a tenant in common.

Even if the property is held jointly with rights of survivorship, the decedent's share of joint property might be needed to pay his taxes or his debts. If a valid claim is filed against the decedent's estate, and there are no other funds available to pay that claim, then the Personal Representative has the right to require that the decedent's share of the joint property be used to pay that claim (NJ 54:34-1(f)) and 17: 16 I-7).

TENANT IN PARTNERSHIP

Another type of joint ownership is partnership property. If the decedent was part of a business partnership and held property as a ***tenant in partnership***, then once he dies, his partner(s) own that property. None of the decedent's creditors can require partnership property to be used to pay his debts, unless the debt was a partnership debt (NJ 42:1-25).

NO MONEY — NO PROPERTY

If the decedent owed money then the bill needs to be paid from assets owned by the decedent — which leads to the next question "Did the decedent have any money in his own name when he died?"

If the decedent died without any money or property in his name, then there is no money to pay any creditor. The only question that remains is whether anyone else is liable to pay those bills. The issue of payment most often arises in relation to services provided by nursing homes. When a person enters a nursing home, he is usually too ill to speak for himself or even sign his name. In such cases, the nursing home administrator will ask a family member to sign a battery of papers on behalf of the patient before allowing the patient to enter the facility. Buried in that battery of papers may be a statement that the family member agrees to be personally responsible for payment to the nursing home.

If the family member refuses to guarantee payment and the patient's finances are limited, then the facility may refuse to admit the patient. If a nursing home accepts Medicare or Medicaid payments, then under the Federal Nursing Home Reform Law, that nursing home is prohibited from requiring a family member to guarantee payment as a condition for allowing the patient to enter that facility (USC Title 42 §1395I-3(c)(5)(A)(ii)). Nonetheless, it is common practice for nursing home, in effect, to say "Either someone agrees to pay for the patient's bill or you need to find a different facility."

Their position is understandable. Most nursing homes are business establishments and not charitable organizations. The nursing home must be paid for the services they provide or they soon will be out of business. For an insolvent patient, the solution to the problem is to have the patient admitted to a facility as a Medicaid patient.

But suppose the decedent had some money when he entered the nursing home and you agreed to guarantee payment to the nursing home?

What if you feel that you were coerced into signing as a guarantor?

Are you now liable to pay the decedent's final nursing home bill if your family member died without funds?

If you are the decedent's spouse, then as explained, under New Jersey law, you are responsible to pay. If you are not the decent's spouse, then an experienced Elder Law attorney will be able to answer these questions after examining the documents that you signed and the conditions under which the patient entered the nursing home.

PAYING THE DECEDENT'S BILLS

If the decedent owed money and he died owning property, belonging to him alone, such as a bank account, securities, or real property, then there may be money available to pay monies owed by the decedent. It is up to the decedent's Personal Representative to pay all valid debts, but to do so the Personal Representative first must gain possession of the decedent's assets. To gain possession of the decedent's assets, there will need to be some sort of probate procedure to determine who is entitled to the decedent's property.

Once the probate procedure begins, all of the decedent's creditors will be given an opportunity to come forward and produce evidence showing how much is owed. The Personal Representative needs to look over each unpaid invoice and decide whether it is a valid bill. The problem with making that decision is that the decedent is not here to say whether he actually received the goods and services now being billed to his estate.

That is especially the case for medical or nursing care bills. An example of improper billing brought to the attention of this author was that of a bill submitted for a physical examination of the decedent. The bill listed the date of the examination as July 10th, but the decedent died on July 9th. Other incorrect billings may not be as obvious, so each invoice needs to be carefully examined.

If the Personal Representative decides to challenge a bill, and is unable to settle the matter with the creditor, then the probate court will decide whether the debt is valid and should be paid.

MEDICAL BILLS COVERED BY INSURANCE

If the decedent had health insurance you may receive an invoice stamped "THIS IS NOT A BILL." This means the health care provider has submitted the bill to the decedent's health insurance company and expects to be paid by them. Even though payment is not requested, it is important that you verify that the bill is valid for two reasons:

➢ LATER LIABILITY

If the insurer refuses to pay the claim, the facility will seek payment from whoever is in possession of the decedent's property, and that may reduce the amount inherited by the beneficiaries.

➢ INCREASED HEALTH CARE COSTS

Regardless of whether the decedent was covered by a private health care insurer or Medicare, improper billing increases the cost of health insurance to all of us. Consumers pay high premiums for health coverage. We, as taxpayers, all share the cost of Medicare. If unnecessary or fraudulent billing is not checked, then ultimately, we all pay.

Special Situation MEDICARE FRAUD

If you believe that you have come across a case of Medicare fraud, you can call the ANTI-FRAUD HOTLINE (800)447-8477 and report the incident to the Office of the Inspector General of the United States Department of Health and Human Services.

HOW TO CHECK MEDICARE BILLING

If the decedent was covered by Medicare, then an important billing question is whether the health care provider agreed to accept Medicare ***assignment of benefits***, meaning that they agreed to accept payment directly from Medicare. If so, the maximum liability for the patient is **20%** of the amount determined as reasonable by Medicare. For example, suppose a doctor bills Medicare $1,000 for medical treatment of the decedent. If Medicare determines that a reasonable fee is $800, then the patient is liable for 20% of the $800 ($160).

Health care providers who do not accept Medicare assignment bill the patient directly. They can charge up to 15% more than the amount allowed by Medicare. If the decedent knew and agreed to be liable for the payment, then his estate may be liable for whatever Medicare doesn't pay. For example, if a doctor's bill is $1,000 and Medicare allows $800, then Medicare will reimburse the decedent's estate 80% of $800 ($640). The doctor may charge the estate 15% more than the $800 ($920) and the estate may be liable for the difference: $920 - $640 or $280.

To summarize:
For health care providers accepting Medicare assignment, the most they can bill the decedent's estate is 20% of what Medicare allows (not 20% of what they bill.)

Those who do not accept Medicare assignment, can bill 15% more than the amount allowed by Medicare. The decedent's estate may be liable for the difference between the amount billed and the amount paid by Medicare.

In either case, if the decedent had secondary health care insurance, then the secondary insurer may be responsible to pay for the difference. If you have a question about Medicare billing call MEDICARE PART B CUSTOMER SERVICE (800) 333-7586.

Special Situation

DENIAL OF MEDICARE COVERAGE

If the health care provider reports to you that services provided to the decedent are not covered by Medicare, or if the facility submits the bill to Medicare and Medicare refuses to pay, then check to see if you agree with that ruling by determining what services are covered under Medicare. See page 47 to get publications on what is (or is not) covered. You can also call the toll free Medicare Hotline (800) 633-4227. English and Spanish speaking operators are available Monday through Friday from 8 a.m. to 4:30 p.m. For the hearing impaired call TTY/TDD call (877) 486-2048.

THE MEDICARE APPEAL

If you believe that the decedent has wrongly been denied coverage, then you can appeal that decision. You can call the New Jersey Bar (732) 249-5000 for a referral to an attorney experienced in Medicare appeals. Some attorneys work ***pro bono*** (literally for the public good, i.e. without charge) but most charge to assist in an appeal. Federal statute 42 U.S.C. §406(a)(2)(A) limits the amount an attorney may charge for a successful Medicare appeal to 25% of the amount recovered or $4,000, whichever is the smaller amount.

SOME THINGS ARE CREDITOR PROOF

Sometimes it happens that the decedent had money or property titled in his name only, but he also had a significant amount of debt. Whether the creditor will be paid may depend on whether the asset is "creditor proof" under New Jersey law:

✧ PERSONAL PROPERTY ✧

If the decedent left a spouse or a child who was living at home then the decedent's clothing and personal property to a maximum value of $5,000 is exempt from the claims of the decedent's creditors (NJ 3B:16-5).

✧ INSURANCE PROCEEDS ✧

If a life insurance policy is payable to a beneficiary (and not the decedent's estate), then regardless of the value of the policy, these monies are not available to pay debts owed by the decedent. The only exception is if the decedent purchased the policy to defraud his creditors. If a creditor can prove that such is the case, then the money paid by the decedent for the policy, plus interest will be paid to the creditor from the proceeds of the policy (NJ 17B:24-6).

✧ RETIREMENT PLANS ✧

Monies held in the decedent's retirement account are exempt from his creditors. This exemption includes private retirement plans and Federal retirement plans established according to 26 U.S.C 401, 403, 408 (IRA accounts) or 409. Monies received by beneficiaries of these plans are exempt from the claims of the decedent's creditors (NJ 25:2-1).

✧ ANNUITIES UP TO $500 PER MONTH ✧

An ***annuity*** is a type of investment in which a person contracts with a company (usually an insurance company) to receive period payments over a period of time. In New Jersey, annuity contracts are exempt from the claims of creditors but only up to $500 per month.

Anything over $500 can be reached by the creditors of the ***annuitant*** (the person receiving the monthly payment). If the decedent owned an annuity contract and the annuity payments go to the decedent's beneficiary, then this creditor protection extends to the beneficiary, provided the decedent did not buy the annuity with the intent of defrauding his creditors (NJ 17B:24-7).

✧ THERE IS A PRIORITY OF PAYMENT ✧

The next thing to consider when paying the decedent's debts, is that not all debts are equal. New Jersey Statute 3B:22-2 establishes an order of priority for payment of claims made against the decedent's estate.

1. FUNERAL EXPENSES

Top priority goes to paying the decedent's reasonable funeral expenses.

2. COST OF ADMINISTRATION

Next in priority are the costs and expenses of the administration of the Probate Estate, including the fees charged by the Personal Representative and his attorney.

3. FEDERAL OR STATE TAXES

If there is a debt or a tax that has preference under Federal law or New Jersey law, then it is third in priority. This includes monies owed for services given to the decedent by the Office of the Public Guardian for Elderly Adults.

4. COST OF LAST ILLNESS

The reasonable medical and hospital expenses of the decedent's last illness are fourth in priority of payment. This includes monies due to people who were caring for him.

5. JUDGMENTS

Judgments entered against the decedent are fifth in priority. The time of their entry establishes priorities between them. For example, if a judgment was entered on June 25, 2000 and another entered on June 26, 2000, then the June 25th judgment must be paid first.

6. ALL OTHER CLAIMS

Other than the priorities established within Class 5, there are no priorities within a given class. For example, suppose the decedent left enough money to pay for his funeral, the probate, with $15,000 left over. If there are no other debts, his beneficiaries will inherit the $15,000.

Suppose instead that he left a hospital bill of $20,000 and a nursing home bill of $20,000 (both Class 4 debts). The $15,000 will be prorated. The hospital and nursing home will each get half. There will be nothing left for any Class 5 or Class 6 creditor. There will be nothing left for any heir.

✧ THERE IS A STATUTE OF LIMITATION ✧

Finally, consider that there is a statute of limitations for bringing a claim against the Probate Estate of the decedent. Any time after the granting of Letters, the Surrogate may order the Personal Representative to give public notice to the decedent's creditors that the creditor has 6 months from the date of the order to present his claim to the Personal Representative.

Once claim is filed, the Personal Representative has 3 months to determine whether the claim is valid. If it is a proper debt to the estate, then it must be paid according to the order of priority as described on the previous page. If the Personal Representative decides that all or part of the claim is not correct he can challenge the claim, then the creditor has 3 months to file a law suit to get an order requiring that the debt be paid. If the creditor does not file within that 3 month period, he loses his right to be paid.

But suppose a creditor comes forward after the 6 months allowed by the court to file claims? If the probate is ongoing and Personal Representative has not distributed all of the assets then the court may decide to allow the creditor to pursue his claim — provided there is enough money in the estate to pay all the creditors that came forward during the 6 month period (NJ 3B:22-4; 3B:22-7; 3B:22-8; 3B:22-10; 3B:22-11; 3B:22-14).

Special Situation

DECEDENT ON MEDICAID

Medicaid is a program that provides medical and long term nursing care for people with low income and limited resources. The program is funded jointly by the federal and state government. Federal law 42 U.S.C. 1396(p) requires the state to recover monies spent from the estate of a Medicaid recipient who was 55 or older when the decedent received Medicaid assistance. The state will seek reimbursement for the cost of nursing home care or for homebased care or for other community based services. Federal law prohibits the state from recovering Medicaid funds until the surviving spouse, and/or disabled child are deceased.

Usually there are no monies to recover from the decedent's estate because to qualify for Medicaid in New Jersey a person may not have more than $2,000 in assets.

Sometimes it happens that a person on Medicaid dies and his estate later receives money perhaps as part of a cash settlement of a lawsuit. In such case, the state of New Jersey becomes a Class 3 creditor (NJ 30:4D-7.2).

☎ LAWYER

DECEDENT LEAVING CONSIDERABLE DEBT

If the decedent died leaving much debt and no property, then the solution is simple. No probate, no one gets paid. But if the decedent had property and died owing a significant amount of money, his heirs may wonder whether they should go through a probate procedure if there will be little, if anything, left after the creditors are paid.

But ignoring this problem might not make it go away. Creditors can be tenacious and use whatever legal strategy is available in order to be paid. For example, if no one starts a probate procedure within 60 days of the decedent's death, a creditor can petition the court to be appointed as the Personal Representative of the estate (NJ 3B:10-8).

Family members may object to having a creditor as a Personal Representative, so there could be a court battle over who has priority to be appointed as Personal Representative. There could be other disagreements regarding whether the claim is valid and should be paid.

Court battles are expensive, emotionally as well as financially. Before you decide to give up your right to be appointed as Personal Representative, consult with an attorney experienced in probate matters for his/her opinion about the best way to administer the decedent's estate.

Suppose you owed money to the decedent? Do you need to pay that debt now that he is dead? That depends on whether there is some written document that says the debt is forgiven once the decedent dies. For example, suppose the decedent lent you money to buy your home. If he left a Will saying that once he dies, your debt is forgiven, then you do not need to make any more payments. If you signed a promissory note and mortgage at the time you borrowed the money from the decedent, then the Personal Representative should sign the original promissory note "PAID IN FULL" and return the note to you. If the mortgage was recorded, then the Personal Representative should sign and record a satisfaction of mortgage.

If you owed the decedent money and there is no Will, or if there is a Will, no mention of forgiving the debt, then you still owe the money, even if you happen to be appointed as the Personal Representative (NJ 3B:10-14). If you borrowed the money from the decedent and his spouse, then you need to pay the debt to the spouse. If you borrowed the money from the decedent only, then the debt becomes an asset to the estate of the decedent, meaning that you now owe the money to the decedent's beneficiaries. If you are one of those beneficiaries, you can deduct the money from your inheritance. For example, suppose your father left $70,000 in a bank account to be divided equally between you and your two brothers. If you owed your father $20,000, then your father's estate is really worth $90,000. Instead of paying the $20,000, you can agree to receive $10,000 and have the $20,000 debt forgiven. Each of your brothers will then receive $30,000 in cash.

Who Are The Beneficiaries? 5

A question that comes up early on is who is entitled to the property of the decedent. To answer the question you first need to know how the property was titled (owned) as of the date of death.

There are three ways to own property. The decedent could have owned property jointly with another person; or in trust for another person; or the decedent could have owned property that was titled in his name only.

In general, upon the decedent's death:

> **Joint Property with rights of survivorship** belongs to the surviving joint owner.
>
> **Trust Property** belongs to the beneficiary of the trust.
>
> Property owned by the **decedent only** belongs to the beneficiaries named in the Will.
> If there is no Will, then the property goes to his heirs according to the New Jersey Laws of Intestate Succession.
>
> NOTE ⇨ If the decedent was married, then his spouse may have rights in his property.

This chapter explains each of these types of ownership in detail.

PROPERTY HELD JOINTLY

Bank accounts, securities, motor vehicles, real property can all be owned by two or more people. If one of the owners dies, then the survivor(s) continue to own their share of the property. Who owns the share belonging to the decedent depends on New Jersey law and how ownership of the property was set up (NJ 17: 16 I-6).

THE JOINT BANK ACCOUNT

If a bank account is opened in two or more names, then each depositor is given a statement of the terms and conditions of the account. The statement will say whether each depositor has authority to make a withdrawal, or whether two signatures are necessary. The statement will also say whether there are rights of survivorship. Unless the statement indicates differently, it is presumed that each joint owner is an equal owner of the account and that there are rights of survivorship.

Once an owner of a joint account dies, the surviving owner is free to withdraw all of the monies from the account. If there are two or more surviving owners, whoever withdraws the funds needs to cooperate to divide the account equitably. The surviving owner(s) also needs to keep in mind that if there is not enough money in the decedent's estate to pay valid claims, then the Personal Representative has the right to require that the decedent's share of the joint account be used to pay those claims. The Personal Representative has two years from the decedent's death to demand monies from the joint account. If no request is made during the two year period, then the surviving joint owner(s) are free to keep the decedent's share of the account (NJ 17:16 I -5 , 17:16 I -7).

JOINTLY HELD SECURITIES

You can determine whether the decedent owns a security alone or jointly with another by examining the face of the stock or bond certificate. If two names are printed on the certificate then the surviving owner can either cash in the security or ask the company to issue a new certificate in the name of the surviving owner. Each state has its own securities regulations. If a security held in two or more names, was registered or purchased in another state, then you will need to contact the company to determine how the account was set up; i.e. with or without rights of survivorship.

If the decedent held securities in a brokerage account, then the name of the owner of that account is printed on the monthly or quarterly brokerage statement. Not all brokerage firms print the name of a joint owner on the brokerage statement so you need to contact the brokerage firm and request a copy of the contract that is the basis of the account. It may be that the account is held jointly, or perhaps the decedent named a beneficiary who now owns the account. The contract will show when the account was opened and the terms of the brokerage account. If you determine that the account is held jointly or for the benefit of someone, then have the brokerage firm forward the necessary forms to make the transfer to the proper owner or beneficiary.

JOINTLY HELD MOTOR VEHICLE

If a motor vehicle is held jointly, the name of each owner is printed on the title to the motor vehicle as a co-owner. For cars held jointly by husband and wife, the surviving spouse becomes the sole owner of the car, but title to the car needs to be changed within 30 days of the death (NJ 39:3-30.3). The procedure for doing so is simple. The surviving spouse needs take the original title and a certified copy of the death certificate to the local motor vehicle office. They will give the spouse an Affidavit of Surviving Spouse (Motor Vehicle form BA 62) to sign. If the car was registered to the decedent spouse, then the surviving spouse will need to have the registration changed as well.

If the title to the motor vehicle is held by two people and they are not husband and wife, then the surviving joint owner does not automatically own the car. The New Jersey Motor Vehicle Services will require Letters or a Surrogate's certificate saying who now owns the decedent's "half" of the car. If the decedent had a Will, then his half goes to the beneficiaries named in the Will. If he died without a Will, then his next of kin own the decedent's share of the car. The certificate of title must be changed to the new owner, in the same way that the title certificate is changed when the car is in the decedent's name only. The next chapter explains how to transfer title to the car.

Again, you have 30 days to make the transfer. But it is important to change title as soon as you are able. You might be able to get a reduced insurance rate if there is only one person insured under the policy. Also, should the surviving owner be involved in an accident, and title has officially been changed, then there is no question that the estate of the decedent is in no way liable for the accident.

NEW JERSEY REAL PROPERTY HELD JOINTLY

The name of the owner of real property is printed on the face of the deed. To determine whether the decedent owned the property jointly with another person, you need to look at the last recorded deed. See page 62 if you cannot locate the deed. The top paragraph of the deed identifies the person who transferred the property, the "Grantor" or "party of the first part," and the person to whom he transferred the property, the "Grantee," or part of the second part. The Grantee is the owner of the property as of the date of the deed. For example:

> "This indenture, made this day, March 15, 2000,
> between ROBERT TRAYNOR, a single man,
> whose address is 123 Main Street, Trenton, NJ 11100,
> party of the first part, hereinafter referred to as Grantor
> covenants and grants to,
> ALFRED CODY, SR. and ALFRED CODY, JR.,
> as JOINT TENANTS WITH RIGHTS OF SURVIVORSHIP, party of the second part, hereinafter referred to as the Grantee ....."

If, as in the above example, the deed identifies the Grantee as the decedent and another as :

JOINT TENANTS OR

JOINT TENANTS WITH RIGHTS OF SURVIVORSHIP

then upon the decedent's death, the surviving tenant(s) own the property. The surviving owner(s) do not need to do anything to establish their ownership, but the decedent's name is still on the deed. If there is a Probate procedure, then when you transfer the property, a title search will reveal that the joint tenant is now deceased. If no Probate is necessary, then you need to keep a certified copy of the death certificate available to present at closing to prove you are the surviving joint owner of the property.

DEED HELD AS TENANTS IN COMMON

If the Grantee of a deed identifies the decedent and another as TENANTS IN COMMON then the decedent's share belongs to whomever the decedent named as his beneficiary in his Will. If the decedent died without a Will, then the New Jersey Laws of Intestate Succession determine who inherits the property. See page 106 for an explanation of the law.

If the deed names two or more people as the Grantee and does not say whether they are "Joint Tenants" or "Tenants In Common" then according to New Jersey Statute 46:3-17, they hold title as Tenants in Common. If property is owned by the decedent as a Tenant In Common, then a probate procedure is necessary. The Personal Representative named in the Will or if no Will, then the next of kin, will need to employ an attorney experienced in probate matters to record a new deed that identifies the rightful owners.

☎ LAWYER — THE AMBIGUOUS DEED

Most deeds clearly state whether there are rights of survivorship. But some deeds can be read two ways. For example, if Ruth White transferred property to her son and daughter and the deed read:
"Ruth White jointly with Ralph White and Susan Peters"
Did Ruth intend that they all be joint tenants? Or did she intend that if one of her children died first, then that child's share would go to the deceased child's estate? Best to consult with an attorney if you have any question about how to interpret the deed.

DEED WITH A LIFE ESTATE

A ***life estate*** interest in real property means that the person who owns the life estate has the right to live in that property until he/she dies. You can identify a life estate interest by examining the face of the deed. If somewhere on the face of the deed you see the phrase RESERVING A LIFE ESTATE to the decedent, then the Grantee(s) now own the property. For example, suppose the granting paragraph of the deed reads:

> PETER REILLY, a single man,
> of Clark County, New Jersey,
> party of the first part,
> for valuable consideration paid,
> does covenant and grant to
> ROSE SMITH, a married woman,
> . . .
> RESERVING A LIFE ESTATE TO THE GRANTOR

Peter Reilly is the owner of the life estate. While he is alive, the Grantee (Rose Smith) has no right to occupy the property. Once Peter dies, Rose owns the property, and is free to take possession of the property or transfer it, as she sees fit.

As with a survivorship tenancy, nothing need be done to establish Rose's ownership of the property, however she needs to keep a certified copy of the death certificate to produce at closing should she later decide to sell or transfer the property.

DEED HELD AS HUSBAND AND WIFE

If the Grantee on the deed is identified as a married couple, for example: TODD AMES AND SUSAN AMES, H/W or

TODD AMES AND SUSAN AMES, HIS WIFE or

TODD AMES AND SUSAN AMES, HUSBAND AND WIFE

then this creates a ***Tenancy by Entirety***. A Tenancy by Entirety is much the same as a Joint Tenancy with rights of survivorship. When one spouse dies, and providing they are married at the time of death, the surviving spouse owns the property 100% (NJ 46:3-17.2, 46:3-17.5).

The decedent's name remains on the deed. As with a survivorship tenancy, the death certificate needs to be recorded so that anyone who is examining title to the property will know that the surviving spouse is now the sole owner of the property.

☎ LAWYER

DIVORCED PRIOR TO DEATH

If the decedent was divorced before he died, the Final Judgment of Dissolution should state how property owned by the couple was divided. If the deed to real property still shows the decedent and his ex-spouse as Tenants by the Entirety, then you need to consult with an attorney, to determine who now owns the property.

☎ LAWYER

OUT OF STATE PROPERTY

This chapter relates only to property owned by the decedent in the state of New Jersey. If the decedent owned property in another state or country, then the laws of that state or country determine who inherits that property. You need to consult with an attorney in that state to determine who owns the property now that the Grantee is dead.

CAUTION

The above discussion on the different types of ownership of real property presumes that you are in possession of the most recent, valid deed. The decedent could have signed another, later, deed. Before you come to a conclusion about who inherits the property it is advisable to have an attorney or a title company do a title search to determine the owner of the property as of the date of death.

BANK/ SECURITY ACCOUNTS

If the decedent held a bank account or security account in his name "in trust for" or "for the benefit of" someone, then once the bank has a certified copy of the death certificate, the bank will turn over the account to the beneficiary (NJ 17: 16 I -5).

If the bank or security account is registered in the name of the decedent "as Trustee under a Trust Agreement," that means the decedent was the trustee of a trust and the bank will turn over that account to the Successor Trustee of the trust. Banks usually require a copy of the trust when the account was opened, so the bank probably knows the identity of the Successor Trustee. If the trust was amended to name a different Successor Trustee, you need to present the bank with a copy of that amendment together with a certified copy of the death certificate (NJ 17:16 I -2(n)).

MOTOR VEHICLE

If the motor vehicle is held in the name of the decedent "as trustee," then the motor vehicle is part of the trust property. The motor vehicle remains in the trust once the decedent trustee dies. The Successor Trustee will need to contact the motor vehicle bureau to have title changed to that of the Successor Trustee.

REAL PROPERTY

If the decedent had a trust and put property that he owned in the trust then the deed may read something like this:

> JOHN ZAMORA and MARIA ZAMORA,
> his wife, of Bergen County, New Jersey,
> for valuable consideration paid, grants,
> with general warranty covenants,
> to JOHN ZAMORA, **Trustee of the**
> **JOHN ZAMORA TRUST AGREEMENT**
> DATED FEBRUARY 26, 2000,
> the following real property
> . . .

Once the Trustee (John Zamora) dies then that property remains in the trust. The trust document may say whether the person who takes John's place as Trustee (the Successor Trustee) should sell or keep the property or perhaps give it to a beneficiary.

If no instruction is given, the Successor Trustee can use his discretion as to what to do with the property. His decision may be affected by laws relating to the administration of trust property in the state where the property is located. If you are a beneficiary of the trust and you are concerned about what the Successor Trustee will do with the property, then it is best to consult with your attorney.

PROPERTY IN DECEDENT'S NAME ONLY

If the decedent owned property that was in his name only (not jointly or in trust for someone), then some sort of probate procedure will be necessary before the heirs can get possession of that property. Who is entitled to the decedent's Probate Estate depends on whether the decedent died with or without a Will. If the decedent died testate, then the beneficiaries of the decedent's property are identified in the Will.

If the decedent died without a Will, then the state of New Jersey provides a Will for him in the form of a set of Laws of Intestate Succession. These laws determine who inherits the decedent's intestate Probate Estate and what percentage of the Probate Estate each heir is to receive once all the bills and costs of administering the probate procedure are paid.

The law recognizes the right of the family to inherit the decedent's property. The law covers all possible relationships beginning with the decedent's spouse.

WHAT'S A SPOUSE?

In this era of people challenging the concept of the family unit, those of a philosophical bent may ponder the meaning of marriage. Is it a union of two people in the eyes of God? Is it even a union? Maybe it is just a contract between two people. The state does not concern itself with such things. If the decedent was a resident of the state of New Jersey and died without a Will, then his property is distributed according to the laws of the state; and the laws of the state of New Jersey determine whether the decedent was married.

MARRIED IN NEW JERSEY

To be married in New Jersey means that a man and a woman have obtained a license to marry from the state, solemnized the marriage by a state or religious ceremony, and then cohabited together as man and wife. New Jersey law prohibits the marriage of people who are related nearer than cousin. Parental consent to marry is required for anyone under 18. If the person is under 16, then court permission is required (NJ 37:1-6).

THE COMMON LAW MARRIAGE

A common law marriage is one that has not been solemnized by ceremony. The couple agree to live together as man and wife, and then publicly hold themselves out as being married. Many states no longer recognize a common law marriage as being valid, and have passed laws to that effect. The state of New Jersey does not recognize a common law marriage that was entered into in the state of New Jersey after December 1, 1939. New Jersey does recognize common law marriages that take place in another state, provided that state recognizes the marriage as being valid (NJ 37:1-10).

SAME SEX MARRIAGES

Vermont is the first state to recognize a same sex marriage, which they refer to as a "civil union." Several other states have passed statutes, specifically denying marital status to couples of the same gender. As of this date, no law has been passed in New Jersey relating to same sex marriage. Judges in New Jersey have ruled that a marriage license can only be issued to those of the opposite sex. *Rutgers Council of AAUP v. Rutgers*, 298 N.J.Super.442 (1997). It remains to be seen what law, if any, the New Jersey legislature will pass on the subject.

If you have any question about the validity of the decedent's marriage, then it is important to consult with an attorney.

If the decedent died without a Will, then his Probate Estate is distributed as follows:

✧ MARRIED, NO CHILDREN, NO PARENT

The New Jersey laws of Intestate Succession provide that if at the time of death the decedent was married and had no surviving ***issue***, i.e., lineal descendants (children, grandchildren, great-grandchildren, etc.), and no surviving parent, then all of his Probate Estate goes to his surviving spouse (NJ 3B:5-3(a)).

✧ MARRIED, NO CHILDREN, SURVIVING PARENT

If at the time of death the decedent was married and had no surviving issue, but he does have a surviving parent, then the spouse gets the first $50,000, and half of whatever is left. The surviving parent(s) get the other half (NJ 3B:5-3(b)).

✧ MARRIED, WITH CHILDREN

If the decedent was married and had surviving issue, all of whom are also those of the spouse, then the spouse gets the first $50,000 and half of what is ever left. The children get the other half. If the decedent had surviving children at least one who is not the issue of the surviving spouse, then the spouse gets half of the Probate Estate and the children get the other half (NJ 3B:5-3(c)(d)).

✧ SINGLE, WITH CHILDREN

If the decedent was not married when he died, but had children, all of whom survive him, then they share equally in the Probate Estate. If one or more of his children do not survive him, but the deceased child left surviving lineal descendents, then the descendents inherit the share intended for the deceased child ***by representation***. New Jersey statute 3B:5-6 defines "representation" as follows:

> When representation is required to effect disposition of an estate, the estate is divided into as many shares as there are surviving heirs in the same degree of kinship and deceased persons in the same degree who left issue who survive the decedent, each surviving heir in the nearest degree receiving one share and the share of each deceased person in the same degree being divided among his issue in the same manner.

If you understood this definition, and you are not a lawyer, then you missed your calling. For the rest of us (even lawyers) it's a head-scratcher. Maybe the best way to explain the rule is through example:

Suppose the decedent was unmarried with 4 children, Ann, Barry, Carl, David. If he dies intestate, and all his children survive him, then each get 25% of his estate.

CHILD WITHOUT DESCENDANTS DIES BEFORE DECEDENT

If Ann dies before her father leaving no descendants, then Barry, Carl and David divide the estate between them and each gets one third.

CHILDREN WITH DESCENDANTS DIES BEFORE DECEDENT

Suppose instead that only Carl and David survived their father. If Ann died leaving 1 child and Barry died leaving 2 children, then the estate is divided into 4 shares — one for each surviving child and one share for each deceased child who died leaving children. Carl and David each get their share, namely Carl gets 25% of the estate and David gets 25%. The share intended for Ann (her 25%) is given to her child. Barry's 25% is divided equally between his two children.

NO CHILD, NO SPOUSE

If the decedent had no spouse or descendant, then his property is divided equally between his parents. If only one of his parents is alive, then all of the property goes to that parent. If neither parent is alive, then the estate goes to the decedent's brothers and sisters in equal shares, by representation. There is no distinction between full blood siblings or half blood siblings. For example, if the decedent had one brother with the same set of parents, and another brother with the same father and a different mother, then both brothers inherit an equal amount (NJ 3B:5-7).

If the decedent had no brothers, sisters, nephews or nieces, then the Probate Estate is divided with half going to the decedent's next of kin on his mother's side, by representation, and the other half going to the decedent's next of kin on his father's side, by representation. (NJ 3B:5-4).

THE STATE: HEIR OF LAST RESORT

If a person dies without a Will and he has absolutely no relations and no stepchildren, then as a last resort, his property goes to the state of New Jersey (NJ 3B:5-5).

WHO DIED FIRST?

New Jersey law requires that anyone who inherits property according to the law of Intestate Succession must survive the decedent by at least 120 hours (5 days). If a relative does not survive by at least 5 days, then that share is distributed as if the person died before the decedent. This rule is not applied if to do so will result in the State of New Jersey inheriting the property (NJ 3B:5-1).

Sometimes it happens that two family members die simultaneously, and no one knows who died first. For example, suppose a father and son die together in a car crash, how is the property distributed in that case? New Jersey statute provides for an orderly distribution of their respective estates. Each person is assumed to have survived the other and the property of each is distributed on that basis. The father's property is distributed as if he survived his son and the son's property is distributed as if he survived his father. For example, if the father had a $10,000 insurance policy with his son as beneficiary and his daughter as alternate beneficiary, then the money will go to his daughter.

If the father and son owned property jointly, then if they die simultaneously, the property is divided with one half going to the estate of the father and the other half to the estate of his son. (NJ 3B:6-2, 6-4, 6-5).

THE AFTER BORN CHILD

If a child was conceived prior to the decedent's death, and born after the death, then the child inherits the same as any other natural child of the decedent (NJ 3B:5-8).

NON-MARITAL CHILD

A child born out of wedlock has the same rights to inherit from his/her natural father as does one born in wedlock, provided any one of the following are true:

- ☑ The decedent signed a declaration that the child is his and filed the document with the local registrar of vital statistics.
- ☑ The decedent married the child's mother and the child is born during the marriage or within 300 days after the marriage ends because of death, annulment or divorce.
- ☑ He openly acknowledges the child as his.
- ☑ Paternity was established by clear and convincing evidence, which may include a court determination of paternity (NJ 9:17-43)

If the decedent denied his paternity, then it will take a court procedure to establish (or disprove) paternity. If you want to establish paternity, then you need to consult with an attorney who is experienced in litigation. If DNA tests need to be conducted, and the family plans to cremate the decedent, you may need to have your attorney move quickly to bar cremation until the matter is settled.

THE ADOPTED CHILD

Even though a child is adopted, the child still has the right to inherit property from his natural parents provided the rights of the natural parents have not been terminated; for example, if one of the child's parents dies, and the child is later adopted by a stepparent, then that child still retains full rights of inheritance from both of his natural parents, and their respective families.

An adopted child has the same rights to inherit property from his adoptive parents, and his adoptive grandparents as does a natural child. New Jersey law places some restrictions on the right of an adopted child to inherit property through representation from certain relatives of the adoptive parents. For example, if the aunt of a deceased adoptive parent dies without a Will, then the adoptive child cannot inherit property from the adoptive aunt by representation (NJ 2A:22-3, NJ 3B:5-9).

If all this seems complicated to you, it is. Even though you now know more about New Jersey's Laws of Intestate Succession, then you ever wanted to know, there is much more to the law. Unless the descent is straight forward, with the decedent leaving a surviving spouse and/or children (all of whom survive him), it is best to consult with an attorney before you decide who is entitled to inherit the decedent's intestate property.

Special Situation

NO SHARE FOR KILLER

If a beneficiary has been convicted of intentionally causing the death of the decedent, then New Jersey law prohibits the killer from profiting from the crime. Property that the killer would have inherited will be distributed as if the killer died before the decedent. If the killer is a beneficiary of a life insurance policy, then the alternate beneficiary will get the insurance proceeds. If there is no alternate beneficiary, then the proceeds go to the decedent's estate (NJ 3B:7-1, 7-2, 7-3).

☎ LAWYER

LAW SUIT FOR WRONGFUL DEATH

If anyone committed a wrongful act against the decedent that caused injury to the decedent or led to his death, then regardless of whether that person is convicted of the crime, the Personal Representative may sue that person for a wrongful death on behalf of the beneficiaries of the decedent's estate. There is a two year statute of limitations, so the suit needs to be brought within that time (NJ 2A:31-1).

WHEN TO CHALLENGE THE WILL

It is not uncommon for a family member to be unhappy with the way the decedent willed his property. If you are tempted to challenge a Will, first consider whether the Will is valid under New Jersey law.

In New Jersey, a Will is presumed to be valid if at the time the decedent made the Will:

- ➢ he was at least 18 years of age
- ➢ he was of sound mind

The decedent is thought to have acted with sound mind:

- ☑ he knew what he was doing (namely making a Will);
- ☑ he knew what property he had;
- ☑ he remembered and understood his relationship to his family members and how they would be affected by his Will;
- ☑ he was not suffering from a delusional mental disorder affecting his ability to distribute his property;
- ☑ he was not being coerced to sign the Will, that is, no one was forcing him sign it.

New Jersey statute requires that the Will be in writing and signed by the person who is making the Will in the presence of two witnesses (NJ 3B:3-1 and 3B:3-2).

The first step in the probate procedure is to have the Probate court determine whether the Will presented is valid. If the Will is in writing and signed by the Will maker in the presence of at least two credible witnesses, and a Notary Public, then there should be no problem in having the Will accepted into Probate. If the Will was witnessed but not notarized, then the court will ask the witnesses to testify that they saw the Will maker sign the Will.

But suppose the decedent wrote out a Will in his own hand and signed it with no one present? Such a Will is called a ***holographic Will.*** Most states refuse to accept a holographic Will into probate. But in New Jersey, the Surrogates' Court will accept a holographic Will into probate, provided it can be proved that the decedent wrote main provisions of the Will himself and then signed the Will (NJ 3B:3-3).

The problem with a holographic Will, in this or any other state, is its authenticity. Because no one saw the decedent sign the Will, it is hard to determine whether the Will was written by the decedent or is a forgery.

If all the decedent left was a holographic Will, then you need to consult with an attorney experienced in Probate matters, to present evidence to the court that the Will does (or does not) qualify as a holographic Will in the state of New Jersey.

THE VERBAL WILL

Picture a death bed scene. The elderly gentleman is surrounded by several family members. In a whisper, just audible enough to be heard, he says:

"Even though I am a wealthy man, I never got around to making a Will. You all have been good to me, but I did want my entire fortune to go to my nephew, Robert. He has been like a son to me."

Do you think Robert can inherit his uncle's estate?

Not in the state of New Jersey, unless:

- ⇨ Someone writes down his uncles's wishes;
- ⇨ The uncle signs the writing, or tells someone to sign it for him;
- ⇨ Two witnesses watch all this and then sign the Will stating that they saw the uncle sign the Will or heard him tell someone to sign the Will for him (NJ 3B:3-2).

Considering that the uncle's relatives will probably inherit the fortune under the laws of Intestate Succession, it is doubtful that Robert is in danger of becoming wealthy at any time in the near future.

THE WILL THAT IS CONTRARY TO LAW

Sometimes a person who is of sound mind, makes a Will, but that Will has the effect of giving a spouse or a minor child less than is required under New Jersey law. One such example is that of Nancy. Hers was not an easy life. She worked long hours as a waitress. She divorced her hard drinking first husband. The final judgment gave her their homestead, $30,000 in securities, and sole custody of their son. After the divorce Nancy had her attorney prepare a Will leaving all she owned to her son, Richard.

Some years later she met and married Harry, a chef at the restaurant where she worked. He moved into her home and they later had a daughter. Richard was 19, and his stepsister 12, when Nancy died after a lengthy battle with cancer.

Nancy did not leave much — her car, her household furnishings, cash and securities worth $50,000, and the homestead, all of which was in her name only.

Before she died, Nancy told Richard, that she had not changed her Will because she wanted him to have all she owned. She said Harry had a good job and she was sure he would take good care of his daughter.

No sooner was the funeral over, when Nancy's son came in and demanded that Harry vacate his mother's home. Harry was furious and went to his attorney.

"I was a good husband to Nancy, supporting and taking care of her all during her long illness. It was me, and not her son, who was at her side when she died. Don't I have any rights? And what about my daughter. Doesn't she have any rights?"

"Your daughter was born after your wife made her Will, so New Jersey statute gives her the right to inherit as much as she would have received had your wife died without a Will. The same applies to you. You have the right to as much as you would have inherited if your wife died intestate. There are a couple of exceptions to the rule. The rule doesn't apply to you or your daughter if your wife provided for you or her daughter outside of the Will.

"No, she didn't give me or my daughter anything before she died."

"You could have given up your right to inherit property from your wife by signing a pre-nuptial or post-nuptial agreement."

"No. I didn't sign anything."

The lawyer continued "The only other exception to the rule is if the Will shows that she intentionally made no provision for you or the children (NJ 3B: 5-15, 5-16) ."

"No, she didn't know me when she made the Will; and the last thing she was thinking of at that time, was having more children."

"In that case, you are entitled to half of your wife's estate and the children will share the other half."

Harry wondered "How can my stepson get his 1/4th of the house that me and my daughter are living in?"

"The house will need to be sold and the proceeds divided."

Harry was concerned "But that means I need to move out of the house."

"Not necessarily, you could have the house appraised and purchase your stepson's share."

Harry said "Richard and I are not even talking to each other. What if Richard refuses to sell me his share?"

The lawyer answered "Then you are back to selling the house."

Harry was still concerned about moving out of the house "Don't I have Dower rights or something?"

The lawyer explained "Dower rights are for widows. Curtesy rights are for widowers. For marriages that took place in New Jersey after May 28, 1980, Curtesy and Dower rights were replaced by the elective share."

"What's an elective share?"

"If your wife made a Will after you were married, and that Will left you less than 1/3 of her estate, not counting her funeral expenses and claims against her estate, then you could ask the court to give you an ***elective share*** of her estate. If your wife gave property away within two years prior to her death, without your consent; and the gift to any one person was more than $3,000, then the elective share would include 1/3rd of the value of that property as well. The elective share doesn't apply in your case because she made her Will before you married. Actually, that's a good thing in your case, because you get a half and not a third (NJ 3B:8-1, 3B: 8-2; 3B: 8-3)."

Harry did receive half of his wife's estate, and his daughter received 25% of the estate. Richard did not fare nearly as well as his mother intended.

No doubt Nancy did not understand what would happen to her estate once she passed on. The Will she left did not accomplish her goal of providing for her son. All it did was cause turmoil and an irreparable rift between Harry and Richard. It didn't need to be that way. Had Nancy known about New Jersey law, she could have consulted with an attorney and set up an estate plan that could have provided for her son, without alienating her husband.

But, the moral of the story, for the purpose of this discussion, is that if you believe that the decedent's Will is not valid or is not drafted according to New Jersey law, then you need to consult with an attorney experienced in probate matters to determine your legal rights under that Will.

Getting Possession Of The Property 6

Knowing who is entitled to receive the decedent's property is one thing. Getting that property is another. As explained in the previous chapter if the decedent held a bank account, or a security or real property jointly with another, or in a trust for someone, then the property now belongs to the joint owner or beneficiary. In most cases, all the beneficiary need do to get possession of the property is produce a certified copy of the death certificate.

If the decedent held property in his name only, then some sort of probate procedure is necessary in order to transfer ownership to the proper beneficiary. In New Jersey, most probate procedures require the assistance of an attorney, but there are a few items that you can obtain on your own. This chapter explains how to get those items and also what to expect should you need to got through a probate procedure.

DISTRIBUTING PERSONAL PROPERTY

Too often, the first person to discover the body will help himself to the decedent's ***personal effects*** (clothing, jewelry, appliances, electrical equipment, cameras, books, household items and furnishing, etc.). Unless that person is the decedent's sole beneficiary, such action is unconscionable, if not illegal.

If the decedent was married and did not have children, then all of the decedent's personal effects belong to his spouse unless he left a Will giving a particular item of personal property to someone else. The decedent may have left a separate writing giving some personal item to someone. Under New Jersey law, a person can leave any of his personal effects (not money) by means of a separate writing, providing the writing was in the decedent's own hand or if the gift was typewritten or written by another, then it was signed by the decedent (NJ 3B:3-11).

If the decedent was not married, then his personal effects should be given to the person appointed as the Personal Representative. The Representative has the duty to distribute the property according to the decedent's Will, or separate writing, or according to the New Jersey Laws of Intestate Succession in case the decedent died without a Will.

If you determine that there is no need for a Probate procedure and the decedent did not have a Will then his next of kin need to divide all of the personal effects among themselves in approximately equal proportions. Most personal effects have little, if any, monetary value. Furniture may be worth less than it costs to ship. In such case, the beneficiaries may decide to donate the personal property to the decedent's favorite charity.

WHAT'S EQUAL?

The decedent's Will or if no Will, then the New Jersey Laws of Intestate Succession may direct that the decedent's personal property be divided equally between two or more beneficiaries. The problem with the term "equal" is that people have different ideas of what "equal" means. Unless there is clear evidence that the decedent's Will meant something else, "equal" refers to the monetary value of the item and not to the number of items received. For example, to divide the decedent's personal effects equally, one beneficiary may receive an expensive item of jewelry and another beneficiary may receive several items whose overall value is approximately equal to that single piece of jewelry.

When distributing personal effects there needs to be cooperation and perhaps compromise, or else bitter arguments might arise over items of little monetary value.

One such argument occurred when an elderly woman died who was rich only in her love for her five children and 12 grandchildren. After the funeral, the children gathered in their mother's apartment. Each child had his/her own furnishings and no need for anything in the apartment. They agreed to donate all of their mother's personal effects to a local charity with the exception of a few items of sentimental value.

Each child took some small item as a remembrance — a handkerchief, a large platter that their mother used to serve family dinners, a doily their mother crocheted. Things went smoothly until it came to her photograph album. Frank, the youngest sibling, said, "I'll take this." Marie objected saying, "But there are pictures in that album that I want."

Frank retorted, "You already took all the pictures Mom had on her dresser."

The argument went downhill from there. Unsettled sibling rivalries boiled over, fueled by the hurt of the loss that they were all experiencing.

It almost came to blows when the eldest settled the argument: "Frank you make copies of all of the photos in the album for Marie. Marie, you make copies of all of the pictures that you took and give them to Frank. This way you both will have a complete set of Mom's pictures. And while you're at it, make copies for the rest of us."

THE SMALL ESTATE AFFIDAVIT

Suppose that the decedent died without a Will and the only thing in his name was a bank account worth $3,000. The proper beneficiary can get possession of these items by giving the person who holds the property an Affidavit. An ***Affidavit*** is a written statement of facts made by someone (the "Affiant") that is signed in the presence of a Surrogate. The Affiant must swear or acknowledge that the facts as stated in the Affidavit are true.

To use the Affidavit, the following facts must be true:

- ☑ The decedent died without a Will.
- ☑ The value of the decedent's estate is not greater than $5,000.
- ☑ If the spouse is the sole heir, then the value of the decedent's estate is not greater than $10,000.
- ☑ No probate procedure is pending.
- ☑ Ten days have passed since the death.

There is a sample Affidavit for the spouse on the next page and a sample Affidavit on the following page if the decedent was single and the Probate Estate $5,000 or less.

AFFIDAVIT PURSUANT TO NJ STATUTE 3B:10-3

STATE OF NEW JERSEY, COUNTY OF ____________________
The Affiant ________________________, first being duly sworn deposes and says:

1. My name and address is:
Name ____
Address ____
____

2. The decedent's name is ______________________________.
and his residence at time of death is ____________________
____

3. The date and place of death of the decedent:
Date ________ Place ___________________________________

4. The decedent died intestate and I am the decedent's surviving spouse. No application or petition for appointment of a personal representative is pending or has been granted in any jurisdiction.

5. The value of the decedent's real and personal assets will not exceed $10,000. Specifically, the nature, location and value of the intestate's real and personal assets are as follows:
____
____
____
____

Sworn to and subscribed before me on this day ______________

____
SURROGATE

AFFIDAVIT PURSUANT TO NJ STATUTE 3B:10-4

STATE OF NEW JERSEY, COUNTY OF ______________________

The Affiant ______________________, first being duly sworn deposes and says:

1. My name and address is:

Name ______________________________________

Address ______________________________________

____

2. The decedent's name is ______________________.
and his residence at time of death is ______________________

____

3. The date and place of death of the decedent:

Date __________ Place ______________________

4. The decedent died intestate. My relation to the decedent is ____________, and I am the decedent's heir. The remaining heirs have consented to me taking possession of the decedent's estate. Their written consent is attached to this Affidavit.

5. No application or petition for appointment of a personal representative is pending or has been granted in any jurisdiction.

5. The value of the decedent's real and personal assets will not exceed $5,000. Specifically, the nature, location and value of the intestate's real and personal assets are as follows:

____

____

____

____

Sworn to and subscribed before me on this day ____________

____
SURROGATE

The Affidavit needs to be filed and recorded in the county where the decedent lived. If the decedent was not a New Jersey resident, then the Affidavit can be filed in the county where the decedent's property is located.

The National Center For State Courts has a Web site that gives information about the court system in each state. You can find the address, phone number, office hours for local court houses. There are even pictures of the court house for some county courthouse listings.

WEB SITE FOR NEW JERSEY STATE COURTS
http://www.ncsc.dni.us/

You will need to sign the Affidavit in the presence of the Surrogate or in the presence of the Clerk of the Superior Court. You may save time if you first call the Surrogate or Clerk of the Superior Court. Some questions you might want to ask are:

How do I get to the Court house?
What is the best time to meet with you?
What documents do I need to bring with me?
How much will it cost to file?
Is a personal check acceptable or do I need to bring cash or a money order?

If you live out of state, then you can call the Surrogate in the county of the decedent's residence, or if the decedent lived out of state, then in the county where the property of the decedent is located. You will need to get the Surrogate's permission to have the Affidavit signed by a Notary or by a court official in your state.

Once the Affidavit is properly filed and recorded, the Surrogate (or Clerk) will give you a copy of the Affidavit marked "TRUE COPY." You can give a copy of the Affidavit to whoever has possession of the decedent's property (bank, securities broker, etc.) and they will turn over the property to you (NJ 3B:10-5).

Whoever takes possession of the property has the responsibly to see to it that the decedent's bills are paid. For example, if monies are owed for the decedent's funeral, then these funds must be used to pay for the funeral. If it later turns out that a full probate procedure is necessary, then whoever took possession of the personal property will need to deliver that property to the Personal Representative or show that the money was used to pay the decedent's valid debt.

As explained on page 85, the spouse can inherit up to $5,000 free from the claims of the decedent's creditors. If the spouse is using the Affidavit to collect more than $5,000 then the spouse must use anything over $5,000 to pay any valid bill owed by the decedent (NJ 3B:10-3).

INCOME TAX REFUNDS

You need to file the decedent's final income tax return (IRS form 1040) by April 15th of the year following the year in which he died. If there is a refund due to the decedent and you are entitled to that money as the beneficiary of the decedent, then you can obtain the refund by filing IRS form 1310 along with the 1040. You can obtain form 1310 from the decedent's accountant, or if he did not have an accountant and you wish to file yourself, then call the IRS at (800) 829-3676 to obtain the proper form. You can obtain instructions, publications and form from the Internal Revenue Service Web site:

IRS WEB SITE

IRS FORMS AND INSTRUCTIONS

http://www.irs.ustreas.gov/prod/forms_pubs/forms.html

IRS PUBLICATIONS

http://www.irs.ustreas.gov/prod/forms_pubs/pubs.html

If you are appointed as Personal Representative, you do not need to file form 1310 because once you file the decedent's final income tax return, any refund will be forwarded to you as Personal Representative. Similarly, a surviving spouse does not need to file form 1310 because the spouse will automatically receive any refund due on their joint income tax return.

THE STATE INCOME TAX REFUND

The decedent's final New Jersey State income tax return needs to be filed at the same time the federal income tax return is filed. If the Personal Representative files the return, then any refund will be given to him to be deposited to the estate account. If no probate procedure is necessary, then the next of kin can file the return. If you need information about filing the final return, you can call the New Jersey Division of Taxation (609) 292-6400 or you can visit their Web site:

NEW JERSEY DIVISION OF TAXATION WEB SITE
http://www.state.nj.us/treasury/taxation

DEPOSITING THE TAX REFUND

If the refund check is sent to the Personal Representative, then he will deposit it to the estate account. If there is no probate procedure and the refund check (or any other check made out to the decedent) is in the name of the decedent, you can deposit the check to the decedent's bank account and then use whatever probate procedure is appropriate depending on the value of the estate. If the decedent does not have a bank account, and died without a Will, and the refund is less than $5,000 you can use the Small Estate Affidavit to get the refund (see page 125).

TRANSFERRING THE CAR

If the decedent owned a motor vehicle, then title to the car needs to be transferred to the new owner and new owner needs to register the car in the state where it will be driven. You may want to limit the use of the car until it is transferred to the beneficiary. If the decedent's car is involved in an accident before the car is transferred to the new owner, then the decedent's estate may be liable for the damage. Having adequate insurance on the car may save the estate from monetary loss, but a pending lawsuit could delay the probate procedure and prevent any money from being distributed to the beneficiaries until the lawsuit is settled.

If the car was held jointly with the spouse, then the spouse can take a certified copy of the death certificate, and the original title to the local Motor Vehicle office. If the car was in the decedent's name only, or if held jointly with someone other than a spouse then it is the Personal Representative's job to transfer the motor vehicle to the proper beneficiary. If the decedent had a Will and he made a specific gift of the car to someone, then the Personal Representative will transfer the car to that person.

If there was no mention of the car in his Will, then the car goes to the ***residuary beneficiaries*** under the Will. A residuary beneficiary is someone who inherits whatever is left of the estate, once any specific gift mentioned in the Will is made and once all the bills and costs of administration have been paid. If the decedent did not have a Will, then the car goes to the decedent's heirs as determined by the New Jersey Laws of Intestate Succession (see page 106).

If the car is in the decedent's name only or held jointly with someone (not his spouse), then in order to transfer the car to the proper beneficiary you will need Letters issued by the Surrogate, or a Small Estate Affidavit. The Small Estate Affidavit is appropriate if the decedent died without a Will and the value of the car is no more than $5,000. Once you have the Affidavit, or Letters from the Surrogate, the Motor Vehicle Services will help you through the process of transferring title to the motor vehicle. You may wish to first call to determine the cost of the transfer and what documents they require. Their in state toll free number is (888) 486-3339. For out of state call (609) 292-6500 or you can get information from their Web site:

NEW JERSEY DEPARTMENT OF MOTOR VEHICLES
http:www.state.nj.us/transportation

TRANSFER WHEN MORE THAN ONE BENEFICIARY

If there is more than one person who has the right to inherit the car, then they all can take title to the car. That may not be a practical thing to do since only one person can drive the car at any given time and if one gets into an accident, then they all can be held liable. The better route is for the beneficiaries to agree to have one person take title to the car. The person taking title will need to compensate the others for their share of the car. In such case the beneficiaries need to come to an agreement as to the value of the car.

DETERMINING THE VALUE OF THE CAR

Cars are valued in many different ways. The ***collateral*** value of the car is the value that banks use to evaluate the car for purposes of making a loan to the owner of the car. Because banks print these values in book form, the collateral value is also referred to as the ***book value*** of the car. If you were to trade in a car for the purpose of purchasing a new car, then the car dealer will offer you the *wholesale* value of the car. Were you to purchase that same car from a car dealer, then he will price it at its ***retail*** or ***fair market value***. Usually the retail price is highest, wholesale is lowest and the book value of the car is somewhere in between.

You can call your local bank to get the book value of the car. It may be more difficult to obtain the wholesale value of the car because the amount of money a dealer is willing to pay for the car depends on the value of the new car that you are purchasing. You can determine the car's retail value by looking at comparable used car advertisements in the local newspaper or over the Internet.

TRANSFERRING THE MOBILE HOME

A mobile home is a motor vehicle, so the methods described can be used to transfer the decedent's mobile home. Before transferring the mobile home you need to find out whether the land on which the mobile home is located was leased or owned by the decedent.

If the decedent was renting space in a trailer park, then you need to contact the trailer park owner to transfer the lease agreement to the beneficiary of the mobile home. If the decedent owned the land under the mobile home, then a probate procedure will be necessary to transfer the land to the proper beneficiary. See page 136 for a discussion of the transfer of real property.

Special Situation

TRANSFERRING THE LEASED CAR

The leased car is not an asset of the estate because the decedent did not own the car. The leased car is a liability to the estate because the decedent was obligated to pay the balance of the monies owed on the lease agreement. The Personal Representative, or next of kin, needs to work out an agreement with the company to either assign the lease to a beneficiary or family member who will agree to pay for the lease — or to have the estate pay off the lease by purchasing the car under the terms of the lease agreement.

Some lenders will allow the lease to be assigned to a beneficiary provided the estate remains liable for the balance of payment. In such cases, it is better to have the beneficiary refinance the car and have the original lease agreement paid in full.

If the remaining payments exceed the current market value of the car, there may be a temptation to hand the keys over to the leasing company. This may not be the best strategy, because the leasing company can then sell the car and then sue the estate for the balance of the monies owed. If the decedent had no assets or if the only assets he had are creditor proof, then simply returning the car may be an option. But if the decedent's estate has assets available to pay the balance of the lease payments, then the Personal Representative needs to arrange to have the car transferred in a way that releases the estate from all further liability.

TRANSFERRING REAL PROPERTY

If the decedent owned real property in his name only, or if the decedent owned property as a Tenant in Common, then a full probate procedure is necessary in order to transfer the parcel to the proper beneficiary. No probate procedure is necessary to transfer New Jersey real property if the decedent held that property:

- ⇨ as the owner of a life estate — or —
- ⇨ jointly with rights of survivorship — or —
- ⇨ as tenants by the entirety (i.e., as husband and wife)

As explained, upon the decedent's death the survivors have full ownership of the property. If there is a probate procedure for other property owned by the decedent, then a title search at the time of transfer will reveal the fact that the joint owner died. If no probate is necessary, then all you need to do is to keep a certified copy of the death certificate so that you will have it ready to present at closing should you decide to sell or transfer the property at a later time.

☎ LAWYER

OUT OF STATE PROPERTY

If the decedent owned out of state property jointly with another, it is important to consult with an attorney in that state to determine what documents, if any, need to be recorded in that state. Some states require a death certificate to be recorded in the county where the property is located. Other states require an affidavit to be recorded stating that the joint owner is deceased. An attorney who is experienced in real property law will be able to explain state law to you.

THE FULL PROBATE PROCEDURE

If the decedent had property in his name only, then a full probate procedure is necessary. The only exception is when the decedent dies without a Will leaving property worth no more than $5,000 (or no more than $10,000 if married) (see page 125). The full procedure can take anywhere from several months to more than a year depending on the size and complexity of the Probate Estate.

The New Jersey probate procedure is not very complex, but there is liability associated with the process and it best that the Personal Representative employ an attorney to guide him through the process. For example, it is the Personal Representative's job to pay the costs of administering the estate and all of the decedent's valid debts. The expenses are paid from the Probate Estate and not from Personal Representative's pocket; but if the Personal Representative makes a mistake then he may be responsible to pay for that mistake. For example, if he pays a debt that did not need to be paid — or if he transfers property to the beneficiaries too quickly and there were still taxes due on the estate, then he may be responsible to pay for such error (NJ 3B:14-35).

Once an attorney is employed, it then becomes the job of the attorney to see to it that the estate is administered properly and without any personal liability to the Personal Representative. The attorney has the right to receive reasonable fees for his services and those fees are a proper charge to the decedent's Estate. The attorney can charge a flat fee as a percentage of the estate or he can charge on an hourly basis. Hourly fees can run anywhere from $175 an hour to $300 an hour depending on the complexity of the case.

APPOINTING THE REPRESENTATIVE

The first step in the Probate procedure is to have someone appointed by the Surrogate as Personal Representative. If there is a Will, the Surrogate will appoint the person named as Executor of the Will. If the named Executor cannot or refuses to serve or if the decedent died intestate, then anyone with priority can file a petition (request) to be appointed. New Jersey statute 3B:10-2 gives an order of priority for appointing a Personal Representative:

1. The surviving spouse.
2. The next of kin entitled to inherit the estate under the New Jersey Laws of Intestate Succession.
3. Anyone who is qualified under New Jersey law, including the decedent's creditors, if no one else wants to serve.

If two people are equally qualified to serve, say the children of the decedent, then the Surrogate usually will appoint the person who is a New Jersey resident. If two people want to serve and they are both equally qualified, the Surrogate can appoint them to serve together as Co-Personal Representatives.

Once Letters are issued to the Personal Representative, he can take charge and settle the decedent's affairs, in most cases without court supervision. New Jersey statute gives the Personal Representative the right to collect the decedent's property, to manage it, to make repairs, to lease, mortgage or sell real property. He has the right to employ accountants, appraisers, attorneys to assist with the probate procedure. And finally, he has the right to distribute whatever is left after all bills and costs are paid to the proper beneficiary (NJ 3B:14-23, 3B:16-3).

YOUR RIGHTS AS A BENEFICIARY

If you are the beneficiary of an estate, then you have certain rights.

✧ RIGHT TO YOUR OWN ATTORNEY

The attorney who handles the estate is employed by and represents the Personal Representative. If the estate is sizeable, then you might consider employing your own attorney to check that things are done properly and in a timely manner. If you are not in a financial position to employ an attorney, then you can do the following things to protect you interests:

✧ RIGHT TO A COPY OF THE WILL

You have the right to receive a copy of the Will and to be notified of the name of the Personal Representative and his attorney. If the decedent died without a Will, then whoever has priority to be appointed as Personal Representative needs to obtain their Letters within 40 days from the date of death. If the person with priority does not come forward within that time then he loses his priority. You should be notified of the appointment within 40 days. If not, you can call the Surrogate in the county of the decedent's residence and inquire as to the status of the case (NJ 3B:10-2).

✧ RIGHT TO DEMAND SUFFICIENT BOND

It doesn't happen often, but every now and again a Personal Representative will run off with estate funds. A bond is insurance for the estate. If estate monies are stolen then the company that issued the bond will reimburse the estate for the loss. The Surrogate will require a bond if the Personal Representative lives out of state, or if the Surrogate has any concern about the safety of the estate funds. If the Surrogate does not require a bond but you have reason to believe that the estate may not be properly administered, then you have the right to ask the Surrogate to require a bond. Before making the request, consider that the cost of the bond is paid by the estate. If real property cannot be transferred without a court order, then it may be sufficient just to cover the value of the personal property (NJ 3B:15-1, 15-4).

✧ RIGHT TO COPY OF INVENTORY

The Personal Representative is not required to file an inventory of the decedent's assets with the court. You can ask the Personal Representative to give you an inventory of everything in the estate, but if he refuses to do so, then you will either need to accept the refusal or go to court and force the issue. The problem with asking the court to require an inventory is the cost. If you require a formal inventory, then the Personal Representative will need to spend more time to administer the estate and he may need to employ appraisers. The appraisers are chosen by the Personal Representative, but must be approved by the Surrogate (NJ 3B:16-3). The Surrogate will want to be assured that the appraisers are both independent and impartial. The cost of preparing the inventory is a charge to the estate, so ultimately, it comes out the pockets of the beneficiaries of the estate.

✧ RIGHT TO COPY OF TAX RETURNS

It is important that you receive copies of all tax returns that the Personal Representative is obliged to file. If the Personal Representative fails to file a return, or fails to pay taxes, or if he under-reports a tax obligation, then after the estate is closed and the Representative long gone, you could later be called on to pay estate taxes out of the proceeds that you receive. Again the Representative is under no duty to give you a copy of the tax returns. But he should have no reason to refuse your request to see the tax returns.

If the Personal Representative resists telling you how he is managing the estate, you can go to court and ask that the Personal Representative give you a full accounting starting with the inventory value of the estate and ending with the amount of money that will be left to distribute after all the bills have been paid. Again, the drawback to requiring a full accounting is the cost to the estate. If the court orders the accounting, then an accountant may need to be employed and that cost is a charge to the estate.

✧ RIGHT OF SPOUSE TO AN ALLOWANCE DURING CONTEST

The surviving spouse and children of the decedent may need to wait until the estate is closed before they can receive any money or property. There is a provision in the law for a spouse (or child) to receive an allowance is when there is a dispute over whether there is a valid Will. In such case, the surviving spouse or child, has the right to ask the Superior Court to be give an allowance from the decedent's estate while the matter is being settled (NJ 3B:3-30).

✧ RIGHT TO APPROVE FEES

The Personal Representative and his attorney are each entitled to a reasonable fee for their services. New Jersey statute has a schedule of reasonable fees for the Personal Representative based on the value of the Probate Estate:

5% on the first $200,000
3 1/2% on sums over $200,000 up to $1,000,000.
2% on sums over one million or any other percentage that the court may allow.

When making the allowance the statute allows the court to consider the Personal Representative's "... actual pain, trouble and risk in settling the estate, rather than in respect to the quantum of the estate." And the court may award additional sums "... upon showing of unusual or extraordinary services." (NJ 3B:18-1, 3B:18-14, 3B:18-16).

In addition, while the probate is ongoing, the Personal Representative is allowed to take an annual fee of anywhere from 1/5% to 1% of the value of the estate, plus another 6% on any income generated by the estate. Income can be generated from interest or dividends, or from any rental property that is part of the estate.

Fees for attorney for the Personal Representative can be as much as those awarded to the Personal Representative. All fees come out of the estate, so you have the right to know how much will be charged. You can ask the Personal Representative to tell you, in writing, how much he intends to charge, and how much he expects to pay his attorney. Again, he is under no legal obligation to reveal these sums to you prior to billing the estate. But if he does disclose proposed fees and you think the fees are unreasonable, then you have the right to negotiate to reduce the amount. If you cannot come to an agreement, then consider consulting with your own attorney to present your concerns to the court.

✧ RIGHT TO RECEIVE INHERITANCE

The Personal Representative can distribute all of the decedent's personal property (money, securities, etc.) 6 months after he has given notice to creditors that the probate is being conducted. If the Surrogate does not require the Personal Representative to give notice to creditors, and the decedent died without a Will, then the Personal Representative may not distribute the estate until a year has passed (3B:23-18).

You may want to check with the Personal Representative to see if notice has been given to creditors. If the Surrogate does not require notice, there is nothing to bar the Personal Representative from giving notice on his own. You might ask the Personal Representative to do so, in order that property can be distributed after 6 months instead of waiting the year.

If the Surrogate has not required that notice be given, the Personal Representative can refuse your request. In that case, you may need to wait out the year. After the year, ask the Personal Representative when you can expect to receive your inheritance. If he is not responsive, then tell him you intend to ask to Court to order for a final accounting and then a distribution. If this doesn't stir him to action, then that is exactly what you may need to do (NJ 3B:23-17).

ASSERTING YOUR RIGHTS

You as a beneficiary may begin to feel that you have a choice of a rock and a hard spot. If you assert all of your rights, then you may significantly increase the cost of administering the estate. Worse yet, when deciding how much to award the Personal Representative, the court may decide that your demands caused the Representative ". . . actual pain, trouble and risk in settling the estate . . ." If the court comes to that conclusion, then the Personal Representative can be awarded even more money than the statutory percentages!

In addition, you may feel uncomfortable being assertive with a Personal Representative, who is your friend or family member, and whom you have known for years. Your family relationship may be more important to you than the money you inherit. In such cases, it may be to your benefit to negotiate and compromise rather than take a hard line approach.

Of course, friend or family member, notwithstanding, if you detect dishonesty or flagrant abuse of power, then you may need to move quickly to protect your interests. Before asserting your rights as a beneficiary, you may want to consult with your own attorney to determine the best way to present your concerns to the court.

THE CHECK LIST

We discussed many things that need to be done when someone dies in the state of New Jersey. The next page contains a check list that you may find helpful.

You can check those items that you need to do, and then cross them off the list once they are done. We made the list as comprehensive as possible, so many items may not apply in your case. In such case, you can cross them off the list or mark them ***N/A*** (not applicable).

Things To Do

FUNERAL ARRANGEMENTS TO BE MADE

☐ AUTOPSY ☐ ANATOMICAL GIFT

☐ DISPOSITION OF BODY OR ASHES

DEATH CERTIFICATE

GIVE COPY TO: ____________________________________

____

NOTICE OF DEATH

PEOPLE TO BE NOTIFIED ____________________________

COMPANIES TO NOTIFY

- ☐ TELEPHONE COMPANY
  - ☐ LOCAL CARRIER ☐ LONG DISTANCE ☐ CELLULAR
- ☐ NEWSPAPER (OBITUARY PRINTED)
- ☐ NEWSPAPER CANCELLED ☐ deposit refund
- ☐ SOCIAL SECURITY
- ☐ INTERNET SERVER
- ☐ TELEVISION CABLE COMPANY
- ☐ POWER & LIGHT ☐ deposit refund
- ☐ POST OFFICE
- ☐ OTHER UTILITIES (GAS, WATER) ☐ deposit refund
- ☐ PENSION PLAN
- ☐ ANNUITY
- ☐ HEALTH INSURANCE COMPANY
- ☐ LIFE INSURANCE COMPANY
- ☐ HOME INSURANCE COMPANY
- ☐ MOTOR VEHICLE INSURANCE COMPANY
- ☐ CONDOMINIUM OR HOMEOWNER ASSOCIATION
- ☐ CANCEL SERVICE CONTRACT ☐ deposit refund
- ☐ CREDIT CARD COMPANIES ____________________________

____

____

Things To Do

REMOVE DECEDENT AS BENEFICIARY OF:

- ☐ WILL
- ☐ INSURANCE POLICY
- ☐ PENSION PLAN
- ☐ BANK OR IRA ACCOUNT
- ☐ SECURITY

DEBTS

PAY DECEDENT'S DEBTS (AMOUNT & CREDITOR)

____

COLLECT MONIES OWED TO DECEDENT (AMOUNT & DEBTOR)

____

TAXES

- ☐ FILE FINAL FEDERAL INCOME TAX RETURN
- ☐ FILE FINAL STATE INCOME TAX RETURN
- ☐ RECEIVE INCOME TAX REFUND
- ☐ FILE ESTATE TAX RETURN

PROPERTY TO BE TRANSFERRED

- ☐ PERSONAL EFFECTS
- ☐ MOTOR VEHICLE
- ☐ BANK ACCOUNT
- ☐ CREDIT UNION ACCOUNT
- ☐ IRA ACCOUNT
- ☐ SECURITIES
- ☐ BROKERAGE ACCOUNT
- ☐ INSURANCE PROCEEDS
- ☐ HOMESTEAD
- ☐ TIME SHARE
- ☐ OTHER REAL PROPERTY
- ☐ CONTENTS OF SAFE DEPOSIT BOX

OTHER THINGS TO DO

____

____

____

Preneed Arrangements 7

Death is a wake-up call because once someone close to us dies we are reminded of our own mortality. Many of us believe that death can be put off, but the inevitable is inevitable. Although we cannot change the fact of our death, we have the power to control the circumstances of our death by making preneed arrangements.

Preneed arrangements can be made so that you are buried in the manner you wish and where you wish. You can make arrangements that direct the kind of medical treatments you want to be given in the event you become seriously ill.

You can legally appoint someone to make your medical decisions in the event that you are too ill to speak for yourself. If you let that person know how you feel about life support systems, autopsies and anatomical gifts then that person will be authorized to act on your behalf and will see to it that your wishes are carried out.

As this chapter will show, it is relatively simple and inexpensive to make such preneed arrangements.

When making burial arrangements for the decedent, you may decide to purchase one or more burial spaces nearby for yourself or other family members.

If the decedent was buried in the family plot, then this is the time to take inventory of the number of spaces left and who in the family expects to use those spaces.

If all of the spaces are taken and if you plan to be cremated, then as explained in Chapter 1, some cemeteries will allow an urn to be placed in an occupied family plot. You can call the cemetery and ask them to explain their policy as it relates to the burial of an urn in a currently occupied grave site or mausoleum.

If this is not an option, and the cemetery of your choice has a columbarium, you might consider purchasing a space at this time.

If you wish to have your cremains scattered, then you need to let your next of kin know where and how this is to be done.

Special Situation

VETERAN OR VETERAN'S SPOUSE

If you are an honorably discharged veteran, you have the right to be buried in a Veterans National Cemetery. You cannot reserve a grave site in advance. If your Veteran spouse was buried in a Veterans National Cemetery then you have the right to be buried in that same grave site unless soil conditions require a separate grave site.

If you wish to be buried in a Veterans National Cemetery, then check on current availability (see page 14 for telephone numbers). Let your next of kin know your choice of cemetery.

To establish your eligibility your next of kin will need to provide the following information:

- the veteran's rank, serial, social security and VA claim numbers
- the branch of service; the date and place of entry into and separation from the service

The next of kin will also need to provide the VA with a copy of the veteran's official military discharge document bearing an official seal or a DD 214 form.

If you wish to be buried in a national cemetery, then make all of these items readily accessible to your family.

If you are financially able, in addition to purchasing a burial space, consider purchasing a Preneed funeral plan. It will be easier on your family emotionally and financially if you make your own funeral arrangements. If you do not have sufficient cash on hand for the kind of funeral you desire, then many funeral directors offer an installment payment plan.

Once you decide on a plan, the funeral director will present you with a contract. The print may be small, but it is worth your effort to read it before signing. If the contract is written in "legalese" then either consult with your attorney before signing it or ask as many questions of the funeral director as is necessary to make the terms of the contract clear to you.

If you are not satisfied with the way a certain section of the contract is written then add an addendum to the contract that explains, in plain English, your understanding of that passage. If you are concerned about something that is not mentioned in the contract, then insist that the contract be amended to include that item.

In particular, check to see whether the contract answers the following questions.

Does the contract cover all costs?

The contract should contain an itemized list stating exactly what goods and services are included in the sales price. Ask the funeral director whether there will be any additional cost when you die. For example, if you have not purchased a burial space, then that cost needs to be factored in. If you made provision for a burial space, then you need to make the funeral director aware of where you have arranged to be buried. If you have not made such provision, then the funeral director can assist you in making burial arrangements.

Is the price guaranteed?

New Jersey law requires that your contract state whether you the contract you sign is a Guaranteed Price Agreement or a Non-Guaranteed Price Agreement. The price for the goods and services chosen under a Non-Guaranteed Price Agreement is not fixed. The cost of the goods and services chosen under such a plan may exceed monies paid. In such case, your representative will need to change the plan to one that is covered by the monies you paid, or pay additional monies for the funeral plan that you have chosen.

If the contract is a Guaranteed Price Agreement, then the funeral firm must provide the good and services as stated in the contract, regardless of when you finally die (NJ 45: 7-85 (4)(c)(i)).

How are your funds protected?

There are two ways to fund a Preneed Funeral arrangement. You can have the monies you pay for the Funeral arrangement placed in a Funeral Trust Account, or you can purchase a Funeral Insurance Policy to fund the plan that you choose. The Funeral Insurance Policy can be a life insurance policy or an annuity that will fund the funeral arrangements at the time of your death.

Should you fund the Funeral arrangement with a Funeral Insurance Policy, then you need to know the terms and conditions of the policy. The policy terms and conditions are separate from the arrangements that you make with the funeral firm. Should and you decide to cancel the funeral arrangements, then that does not cancel the Funeral Insurance Policy, nor does it mean that you will receive a refund of the policy premiums, unless your policy provides for a refund (NJ 45:7-86).

If you are paying the Funeral Insurance Policy on an installment basis, then you need to know the penalty should you fail to make payment. And once the policy is paid, they need to disclose the cost to you should you decide to cancel the Funeral Insurance Policy.

FUNDS PLACED IN FUNERAL TRUST ACCOUNT

Your contract may provide that the monies paid for your Preneed Funeral Arrangement will be held the funeral firm's trust fund. New Jersey law requires that the funds be placed in the trust within 30 days of receipt (NJ 2A:102-13). If you go this route, then have the funeral firm agree to furnish you proof of the deposit and have them promise, in writing, to notify you should they decide to change banks.

Under New Jersey law, you have the right to request that your funds be placed in a Pooled Trust Account in a bank of your choice. The monies will be held on deposit together with interest until the contract is performed by the funeral firm. You have the right to immediately withdraw any monies from the Pooled Trust Account. You also have the right to an annual statement of how much principal and accrued interest there is in the account. The Trustees of the account have the right to charge a commission on the account, so you need to be aware of how much that will cost (NJ 3B:11-16).

Regardless of whether your funds are held in the funeral firm trust account or in a Pooled Trust Account, you need to know what penalties will be imposed should you or your heirs decide to revoke the Preneed Funeral Agreement.

CHANGING TO AN IRREVOCABLE CONTRACT

New Jersey statute requires that all Prepaid Funeral Agreements be revocable by the person who purchases the plan during his lifetime or by his Personal Representative or heirs once he is deceased (NJ 45:7-85). There is an exception to the rule. People who apply for Medicaid, Supplemental Security Income ("SSI") or other public assistance program cannot qualify for these programs if their assets exceed a given amount (usually $2,000). A revocable contract is considered to be an asset because the person can cash it in. If the contract is irrevocable, then it does not count as an asset and does not affect a person's ability to qualify for the program. New Jersey statute allows a person to purchase an irrevocable Prepaid Funeral Plan if that person reasonably expects to be applying for a public assistance program within six months (NJ 2A:102-16.1)

If you purchase a revocable contract and then later need to apply for any of these programs you may need to have the contract changed to one that is irrevocable. Check to see that your contract allows you to make such a change without any penalty to you.

Is the funeral firm reputable?

Of course all of these safeguards may fail if you are not doing business with a reputable funeral firm. It is prudent to take the time to check on the firm by calling the investigation division of the State Board of Mortuary Science at (973) 504-6425. Ask whether the funeral firm is licensed; how long they have been in business and if any complaints have been filed against them.

Can the plan be changed after your death?

Your Personal Representative, or your next of kin, can revoke the contract after your death and they may need to do so because:

- your body is missing or cannot be recovered
- you were buried by another facility because your heirs were unaware of your Preneed contract
- you died in another country and were buried there.

But suppose your heirs just want to change the plan to one different from what you chose? Funeral firm generally a allow heirs to:

- purchase a more expensive plan and paying the difference
- change to a lesser plan and receive a refund.

You might want to check whether the contract offered by the funeral firm addresses the issue of making changes to the contract after your death.

You may wonder why anyone would think of changing the decedent's funeral plan, but consider that in today's market, it is not uncommon for a Preneed contract to cost several thousand dollars. A top end funeral complete with solid bronze casket can cost upwards of $40,000.

And there may be other motivations. Consider the case of Mona, a difficult woman with a personality that can only be described as "sour." Her husband deserted her after four years of marriage leaving her to raise their son, Lester, by herself. Once Lester was grown, Mona made it clear to him that she had done her job and now he was on his own. Lester could have used some help. He married and had three children. One of his children suffered with asthma and it was a constant struggle to keep up with the medical bills.

Mona believed in being good to herself. She did not intend to, nor did she, leave much money when she died. She knew that Lester would not be able to afford a "proper" burial for her, so she purchased a funeral plan and paid close to $18,000 for it. She was pleased when the funeral director told her that the monies would be kept safely in a trust fund until the time they were needed.

Lester was not familiar with New Jersey law, so when Mona died he asked an attorney at the Legal Aid office to determine whether the Preneed contract was revocable.

It was.

You know the ending to this story.

If you are concerned that you get the exact type of funeral that you want, with no changes, then you might consider purchasing a life insurance policy payable to the funeral firm. Your contract with the funeral firm should state that the money from this policy is to be used to purchase the exact type of funeral as specified in the contract.

If you think you may move from your present location and do not wish to commit to a single funeral firm, then consider purchasing a life insurance policy to fund your funeral and have it paid to a trusted friend or family member. It is important that the person who is to receive the insurance funds clearly understands why he/she is named as beneficiary of the policy.

It is equally important that the beneficiary agree to use the monies for the intended purpose. It isn't so much that a family member is not trustworthy as it is that they may not understand what you intended — especially in those cases where other funds are available to pay for the funeral. Too often insurance funds are left to a sibling who then refuses to contribute to the cost of the funeral saying in effect "Dad wanted me to have this money — that's why he left it to me."

To avoid a misunderstanding, put it in writing. It need not be a formal contract. It could be something as simple as a letter to the insurance beneficiary, with copies to your next of kin. The next page contains a sample letter.

Dear Romita,

I purchased a $20,000 insurance policy today naming you as beneficiary of the policy. As we discussed this money is to be used to pay for the following:

- *my funeral and grave site*
- *my headstone*
- *perpetual care for my grave*
- *airfare for each of my grandchildren to attend the funeral*
- *dinner for the family after the wake*
- *lunch for the family after the funeral*

If there is any money left over, please accept it as my thanks for all the effort spent on my behalf.

Love,
Dad

P.S. I am sending a copy of this letter to your brother so that he will know that all arrangements have been made.

Whether or not you arrange to pay for your burial or funeral, you need to let your next of kin know your feelings about the burial procedure. Let your family know whether you wish to be cremated or buried. If you wish to have a religious service, then let your family know the type of service and where it is to be held. Let the family know where you wish to be buried, or if you intend to be cremated, then where to place the ashes.

AUTOPSIES

As discussed in Chapter 1, some autopsies are optional. If you have strong feelings about allowing an optional autopsy or not allowing the procedure, then let your family know how you feel.

ANATOMICAL GIFTS

If you wish to make an anatomical gift, you can make that donation by completing a donor card or by letting your family know that you wish to make a donation of some or all of your body parts. Donor cards are available at your local driver's license office.

If you are aged, and in poor health, the local Organ Procurement Organization will probably not consider your body for transplantation of body parts, but you can still donate your body for education and research. If you wish to make such as donation, call or write to any of the schools mentioned on page 6. They will forward a Dedication Form to you along with information on the subject. As discussed in Chapter 1, there will be a charge to your estate for the cost of shipping to the school, so you need to give your family instructions about what to do in the event that you die far from home.

If you do not wish to make an anatomical gift, then let your family know how you feel. Of course, there are problems with just telling someone how you feel about your burial arrangements, autopsies, and anatomical gifts:

YOU TELL THE WRONG PERSON

The person you confide in may not be present when the arrangements are made. For example, if you tell your spouse what arrangements to make then he/she may die before you do — or you could die simultaneously in a car or plane crash.

You may tell someone who does not have authority to carry out your wishes. That was the case with James. Once his wife died, he moved to a retirement community where he lived for 15 years until his death. James had two sons who lived in different states. Although he loved his sons, he had difficulty talking to either of them about serious matters. It was easier for him to talk with his friends in the retirement community. They often spoke about dying and how they felt about different burial arrangements. James would reminisce about his youth and growing up in a farming community in the plains state of Kansas. "I was happy and free. Out there you had room to breathe. It would be nice to be buried there — peaceful and spacious."

When he died, his friends told his sons about their father's desire to be buried in Kansas. They met the suggestion with scepticism and pragmatism:

"Dad didn't say anything like that to me."

"It would cost us double, if we had to arrange for burial in another state. I'm sure he didn't have that kind of expense in mind."

THE PERSON DOES NOT CARRY OUT YOUR WISHES

The person you tell may not understand what you said or perhaps they hear only what they want to hear. An example that comes to mind is the mother who constantly complained that she felt like a burden to her children. She would often say "When I die, just burn my body and throw my ashes out to sea." Her children paid no attention. When she died she was given a full funeral and buried in a local cemetery. They never asked, nor did they consider, that their mother might really did want to be cremated.

WHO WANTS TO TALK ABOUT IT?

For many people the main problem with telling someone what to do when you die is talking about your death. It may be an uncomfortable, if not unpleasant, subject for you to bring up, and for your family to discuss. If this is the case, then consider putting the information in writing and give the instructions to the person who will have the job of carrying out your wishes.

You can legally appoint someone to be your ***Health Care Representative*** by signing a document called an ***Advance Directive for Health Care***. You can give your Health Care Representative authority to make your medical decisions in the event that you are too ill to make those decisions yourself. You Advance Directive for Health Care can also contain a ***Instruction Directive*** such as a ***Living Will*** that tells whether you do (or do not) want life support systems to be used in the event that you are dying and there is no hope for your recovery. To be valid in the state of New Jersey, the Advance Directive for Health Care must be signed, dated and witnessed by two people, neither of whom are your Health Care Representative. Instead of two witnesses, you can sign the Advance Directive in the presence of a Notary Public (NJ 26:2H-55, 26:2H-56).

Various religious and civic organizations offer literature and sample forms of an Advance Directive for Health Care. You can have your attorney draft an Advance Directive especially designed to meet your needs.

You may be thinking "Why bother with an Advance Directive for Health Care? I probably will never need anyone to assist me. And even if I did, my family will tell the doctor what I want."

That was George's thoughts exactly, even though his attorney advised him differently:

"George, you are a man of substantial wealth. You should consider making provision for the care of your property in the event that you take sick. You also should appoint someone to make your medical decisions in the event that you are too sick to make them yourself. New Jersey law gives the person you chose priority in making your health care decisions. If you don't appoint someone, then any, and all, of your family members have the right to assist with your health care decisions (NJ 26:2H-61, 26: 2H-64).

Your third wife Loretta is a lovely lady, but she and your two sons are always at odds. You should appoint someone as your Health Care Representative to make your medical decisions when you can't. And you should give specific written instructions about what care you wish in the event that you are terminally ill."

"You mean sign a Living Will?"

The attorney explained "The Living Will tells your Health Care Representative whether you do, or do not, want life-sustaining medical intervention in certain specific cases, such as if you are in a coma with no hope of recovery."

George said he would think about it. But he didn't.

The attorney's advice turned out to be prophetic. George suffered a stroke while driving a car. His injuries from the accident combined with the severity of the stroke made for a bleak prognosis. The doctors said George would die unless they put him on a ventilator and inserted a feeding tube. Even with life support systems, it was not expected that he would ever come out of the coma.

Loretta told the doctors "Let's try everything to keep him alive."

George's sons did not see it that way. "Why torture him with needles and tubes? Let him pass on peacefully."

George never signed a Living Will, so no one knew how he felt about artificial life support systems. He never appointed a Health Care Representative, so the doctors didn't know who George would have wanted to speak on his behalf. The doctors requested that the matter be brought before the court and let a judge decide the matter.

Loretta petitioned the court to be appointed as George's guardian. So did his children. The court battle over who was to be George's guardian was bitter (and expensive). Before Loretta and George married they signed a prenuptial agreement. The agreement provided for each to give up all rights to inherit property from the other. Loretta had little money of her own. The children accused Loretta of thinking of her own best interest and not that of their father. If George were to die, Loretta would be on her own.

George was a wealthy man, but he was not overly generous with his children. His sons were married and raising their own families. Without any help from their father, each was struggling to support his family. Loretta accused the sons of being anxious to get their substantial inheritance.

The judge ruled that each of the parties had a conflict of interest and could be prejudiced by his/her own circumstances. He appointed a professional, independent, guardian to make medical decisions for George. The guardian conferred with the doctors and determined that it was futile to continue life support systems.

George died.

Everyman's Estate Plan 8

The first six chapters of this book describe how to wind up the affairs of the decedent. As you read those chapters, you learned about the kinds of problems that can occur when someone dies. It is relatively simple for you to set up an estate plan so that your family members are not burdened with similar problems. An ***estate plan*** is the arranging of one's finances to reduce (if not eliminate) probate costs and estate taxes, so that your beneficiaries inherit your property quickly and at little cost.

If you think that only wealthy people need to prepare an estate plan, you are mistaken. Each year, heirs of relatively modest estates, spend thousands of dollars to settle an estate. A bit of planning could have eliminated most, if not all, of the hassle and cost suffered by those families.

The suggestions in this chapter are designed to assist the average person in preparing a practical and inexpensive estate plan, so we have named this chapter EVERYMAN'S ESTATE PLAN. Once you create your own estate plan, you can rest assured that your family will not be left with more problems than happy memories of you.

AVOIDING PROBATE

TRUE OR FALSE?

( ) If you have a Will, it must be probated.

( ) If you don't have a Will, then probate is necessary.

( ) Probate is necessary if the decedent owned anything worth more than $5,000.

If you answered true to any of the above, then go back and read chapters 5 and 6.

Hopefully the reader will forgive the authors' regression to the role of educator (or maybe pedantic). The point that we were attempting to make is simply:

> Whether or not a probate procedure is necessary has nothing to do with whether there is a Will, or even how much money is involved, the determining factor is how the property is titled (owned).

There are three ways to title property:

- ✧ Jointly with another
- ✧ In trust for another
- ✧ In your name only.

In general, property held jointly or in trust goes directly to the intended beneficiary without the need for Probate. Property held in the decedent's name only may need to be probated.

In this chapter we explore the pros and cons of titling property in each of the three ways, beginning with holding property jointly with another.

OWNERSHIP OF BANK ACCOUNTS

You can arrange to have all of your bank accounts set up so that should you die, the money goes directly to a beneficiary. For example, suppose all you own is a bank account and you want whatever you have in this account to go to your son and daughter when you die. You might think that a simple solution is to put each child's name on the account, but first consider the problems associated with a joint account:

⮽ POTENTIAL LIABILITY

If you hold a bank account jointly with one of your adult children and that child is sued or gets a divorce then the child may need to disclose their ownership of the joint account. In such a case, you may find yourself spending money to prove that the account was established for convenience only and that all of the money in that account really belongs to you.

⮽ OVERREACHING

If you set up a joint account with your child so that the child has authority to withdraw funds from the account, then funds may be withdrawn without your authorization. If you open a joint account with two of your children, then after your death the first child to the bank may decide to withdraw all of the money and that will, at the very least, cause hard feelings between them (NJ 17:16 I-8, 17:16 I-9).

⮽ THE MINOR CHILD

In New Jersey, a minor can own a savings or checking account or to lease a safe deposit box in the child's name only or jointly with another (NJ 17:9A-215; 46:39-3). But if you make a minor the joint owner of your account, would you want the child to be able to remove money from your account? Would you want the minor to be able to go to the bank and withdraw everything in your safe deposit box?

Because of these inherent problems, you might want to hold the funds so that your beneficiary does not gain access to the monies until and unless you die. There are three ways to do so: the "in trust for" account, the "pay on death" account and the "transfer on death" registration.

THE IN TRUST FOR ("ITF") ACCOUNT

You can direct a financial institution to hold your account ***in trust for*** ("ITF") one or more beneficiaries that you name. Your contract with the bank will state that the beneficiary does not have access to the account until and unless you die.

THE PAY ON DEATH ("POD") ACCOUNT

You can have a contract with the bank that directs the bank to ***pay on death*** ("POD") all of the money in the account to one or more beneficiaries that you name.

With both the ITF and POD account:

- ⇨ The beneficiary does not have access to the account until the owner of the account dies.
- ⇨ During his lifetime the owner of the account is free to change beneficiaries without asking the beneficiary's permission to do so.

Your contract with the bank can contain specific instructions about how the money is to be distributed in the event that the beneficiary of the account dies before you do (NJ 17:16 I-4).

You can open an account with PAY ON DEATH instructions to give the money to your child when you die, and if the child dies before you, then to your grandchildren in equal shares. For example:

Eldon Connors POD Betty Connors LDPS

which is short-hand for:
"ELDON CONNORS is the owner of the account. On his death, pay the money in the account to BETTY CONNORS, but if she dies first, then give it to her lineal descendants in equal shares, per stirpes."

The term "per stirpes" means the same as does the term "by representation" (see page 107).

There may be times when you wish to hold an account jointly (say with your spouse) and not have a beneficiary inherit the account until you both die. For example:

ELDON CONNORS and LORRAINE CONNORS,
as Tenants by the Entirety
POD BETTY CONNORS LDPS

(NJ 3B:30-11, 3B:30-6).

THE TRANSFER ON DEATH REGISTRATION

The New Jersey law for securities is similar to the statute for banks. You can instruct the holder of the security to TRANSFER ON DEATH ("TOD") to a named beneficiary once you die. As with the Pay-On-Death account, the Transfer-On-Death designation has no effect on the ownership of the security until the owner of the security dies. The security can be held jointly with another with instructions that should one of the owners die, the other becomes the sole owner and once you both die, the security is to be transferred to a beneficiary. For example, you can hold a securities account as follows:

TIM REILLY and OLIVIA REILLY, husband and wife
TOD STUART REILLY

When both of their parents die, Stuart will inherit the securities account. Should Stuart die before his parents, then the securities account will belong to the estate of the last owner to die (NJ 3B:30-3, 30-7, 3B:30-8).

GIFT TO MINOR

At the beginning of this chapter, we identified three problems with a joint account: potential liability if the joint owner is sued; overreaching by the joint owner, and holding an account jointly with a minor. The P.O.D, TOD and "in trust for" account each solve the problem of potential liability and overreaching, but if the beneficiary of such account is a minor, there still is the concern of allowing a child access to a significant amount of money. There is no problem if the gift you make is no more than $5,000 in value. For example, if you hold a POD account and you die before the beneficiary is 18, then the bank will forward the inheritance to the parent or guardian of the child, or whoever has custody of the minor. If the minor is married, then New Jersey law allows the funds to be given directly to the child. For amounts over $5,000, the Surrogate's court will need to appoint a guardian to care for the child's property until the child reaches 18 (NJ 3B:12-6, 3B:12-12, 3B:12-54).

Guardianships are expensive to set up and to maintain. There are several ways to avoid the problem of having a guardian appointed to care for property inherited by a child and we will discuss those methods later in this chapter. If you wish to make a gift to a child at this time an have it held for the benefit of the child, then you can appoint someone to be the Custodian of the gift under the New Jersey Uniform Gifts to Minors Act. This law is designed to protect gifts made to a minor. It is appropriate to use this method is you want to give a child a gift of a security or a life insurance policy, or an interest in a partnership or even tangible property such as an expensive painting. Once the gift is made it becomes irrevocable, so this method is not appropriate unless you are sure that you want the child to have the gift once he/she reaches maturity (NJ 46:38-17).

To make a gift under the New Jersey Uniform Gifts to Minors Act, you will need to name a trusted relative or friend or even a financial institution to be the Custodian of the gift. For example, if you wish to make a gift of an insurance policy on your life, with a financial institution as Custodian, then the owner of the policy can be listed as "ABC BANK as custodian for ____________ (name of minor) under the New Jersey Uniform Gifts to Minors Act." If you die and the child is an adult, then the Bank will give the proceeds of the insurance policy to the child. If the child is minor, then the Custodian will hold the insurance proceeds for the benefit of the child until the child reaches 18 or any other age you direct between the ages of 18 and 21.

The Custodian will invest and manage the property and use as much money as the Custodian thinks necessary for the use and benefit of the child. The Custodian can decide not to use any of the money and just keep it invested till the child reaches maturity. If the parent or guardian of the child, or even the child, if he/she is over 14, are opposed to such action, they can ask the court to order an accounting of the funds and also to order that the monies be used for the care of the child.

Whoever serves as Custodian has a right to be paid for serving in that capacity. Before choosing someone you should check to see whether they want the job and if so, then how much they will charge (NJ 46:38-15, 46:38-27 46:38-28, 46:38-34).

NOTE: The New Jersey legislature has made changes to the Uniform Gifts to Minors Act to take effect in 2007. The new law will be called the New Jersey Uniform Transfers to Minors Act. Any gift made under the old law will still be valid (NJ 46:38-16, 46:38-38, 46:38-41, 46:38A-57)

OWNERSHIP OF REAL PROPERTY

As explained in Chapter 5, if you own real property together with another, then who will own the property upon your death depends on how the Grantee is identified on the face of the deed. If you compare the Grantee clause of the deed to the examples on pages 94 through 101 you can determine who will inherit that property should you die. If you are not satisfied with the way the property will be inherited, then you need to consult with an attorney to change the deed so that it will conform to your wishes.

If you own the property in your name only, then once you die, there will need to be a probate procedure to determine the proper beneficiary of that parcel of land. If your main objective is to avoid probate, then you can have an attorney change the deed so that once you die, the property descends to your beneficiary without the need for probate. As with bank and securities accounts there are different ways to do so, each with its own advantages and disadvantages.

JOINT OWNERSHIP

You can have your deed changed so that you and a beneficiary are joint owners with rights of survivorship. If you do so then should either of you die, the other will own the property 100%. That avoids probate but you will not be able to sell that property during your lifetime without the beneficiary's permission. And if the beneficiary gives permission and the property is sold, the beneficiary will have the legal right to half of the proceeds of the sale.

CAUTION GIFT OF HOMESTEAD

Some people think it a good idea to simply transfer their homestead to their children to avoid probate, but continue to live there. But this just creates a new set of problems:

⌧ RISK OF LOSS

If you transfer your homestead to a beneficiary it could be lost if the beneficiary runs into serious financial difficulties or gets sued. This is especially a risk if your child is a professional (doctor, nurse, accountant, financial planner, attorney, etc.). If your child is found to be personally liable for damages, then the house could become part of the settlement of that law suit.

If your child is (or gets) married, then this complicates matters even more so. If the child is divorced, the property will need to be included as part of the settlement agreement. This may be to your child's detriment because the child may need to share the value of the property with his/her ex-spouse. If you do not transfer the property, then it cannot become part of the marital equation.

⌧ POSSIBLE LOSS OF GOVERNMENT BENEFITS

If you transfer property, then depending upon the value of the transfer, you could be disqualified from receiving Medicaid or Supplemental Security Income ("SSI") benefits for up to 3 years from the date of transfer. The federal and state rules that determine the period of ineligibility are complex. If nursing care may be an issue in the future, then it is best to consult with an Elder Law attorney to prepare a Medicaid Estate Plan.

⌦ LOSS OF HOMESTEAD TAX REBATE

If you put the deed in the beneficiary's name and that property is your homestead, then any reduction in taxes you may be entitled to receive under the NJ SAVER rebate program or as a disabled or senior citizen, or as a veteran, may be lost. It could cost more money in taxes to continue to live in your own home.

It may be possible to avoid losing your homestead tax rebate by transferring the property to a beneficiary and keeping a LIFE ESTATE for yourself. But, as with joint ownership you will not be able to sell the property during your lifetime without the permission of all of the people you named as Grantee on the deed; and if you sell the property each Grantee is entitled to some portion of the proceeds of the sale (NJ 54:4-8.17, 54:4-8.41, 54:4-8.58).

TAX CONCERNS FOR REAL PROPERTY TRANSFERS

Before you make a real estate transfer be it joint interest, life estate or outright gift, you need to consider the tax consequences of the transfer:

⌧ POSSIBLE CAPITAL GAINS TAX

If you gift your homestead to your child and continue to live there until you die, then when the child sells the property there might be a capital gains tax. The child will be taxed on the increase in value from the day <u>you</u> bought the property.

If you don't transfer your home and the child inherits the property, he/she inherits it at the market value as of your date of death. The child can sell the property at that time without any tax consequence.

⌧ POSSIBLE GIFT TAX

If the value of the transfer is worth more than $10,000 you need to file a gift tax return. For most of us, this is not a problem because no gift tax need be paid unless the value of the property (plus the value of all gifts in excess of $10,000 per person, per year, that you gave over your lifetime) exceed an Exclusion amount as set by the Federal government. Once you die, all the money in your estate is added to the amount gifted during your lifetime and estate taxes will be paid on any value above the Exclusion amount. Congress is discussing doing away with estate taxes altogether, but as of this writing the Exclusion amount is $675,000 and is scheduled to increase each year until the year 2006 (see schedule on page 35).

If your estate is in that tax bracket, then you need to be aware that you are "using up" your tax credit.

☎ LAWYER OUT OF STATE PROPERTY

Each state is in charge of the way property located in that state is transferred. If you own property in another state (or country) then you need to consult with an attorney in that state (or country) to determine how that property will be transferred to your beneficiaries once you die. Most state laws are similar to New Jersey, namely, property held as JOINT TENANTS WITH RIGHTS OF SURVIVORSHIP or a LIFE ESTATE INTEREST go to your beneficiary without the need for probate.

If you own property in another state in your name only, or as a TENANT IN COMMON, or if you hold property jointly with your spouse in a community property state, then a probate procedure may need to be held in that state. If it is necessary for your heirs to have probate procedure in New Jersey, then they will need an ancillary (secondary) procedure in the state in which the property is located. This could have the effect of doubling the cost of probate to your heirs.

Still another problem is the matter of taxes. In addition to paying for a second probate procedure, your heirs may need to pay inheritance taxes in the state where the property is located as well as in New Jersey. Your heirs may need to file a tax return in two states. This may double the cost of the accounting fees.

You may wish to consult with an attorney for suggestions about how to set up your estate plan to avoid such problems.

A TRUST MAY BE THE SOLUTION (OR NOT)

As we have seen, many of the ways to avoid probate involve methods with undesirable trade-offs. One way to avoid some of these potential problems is to set up a ***Inter Vivos Trust*** (also known as a ***Living Trust***). A Living Trust is operational during your lifetime and that can be used upon your death, to distribute your property, as you wish, and without the need for probate. You may have been encouraged to set up such a trust by your financial planner, or attorney, or accountant. Even people of modest means are being encouraged by these professionals to use a trust as the basis of their estate plan. But trusts have their pros and cons. But before getting into that, let's first discuss what a trust is and how it works:

SETTING UP A TRUST

To create a trust, an attorney prepares the trust document in accordance with the client's needs and desires. We will refer to the person who signs the document as the ***Trustor*** or ***Settlor.*** If the ***Trustor*** also funds the trust, then he is also referred to as the ***Grantor.*** We will refer to the inter vivos trust as the "Living Trust" or just the "Trust" and the person setting up the trust as the "Grantor." The trust document identifies who is to be the Trustee (manager) of property placed in the trust. Usually the Grantor appoints himself as Trustee so that he is in total control of property that he places into the Trust. The trust document also names a Successor Trustee who will take over the management of the trust property should the Trustee become disabled or die.

Once the trust document is properly signed, the Grantor transfers property into the trust. The Grantor does this by changing the name on the account from his individual name to his name as Trustee. For example, if ELAINE RICHARDS sets up a trust naming herself as trustee, and she wishes to place her bank account into the trust then all she need do is instruct the bank to change the name on the account from ELAINE RICHARDS to:

ELAINE RICHARDS, TRUSTEE of the ELAINE RICHARDS TRUST AGREEMENT DATED JANUARY 12, 2000.

Once the change is made, all the money in the bank account becomes trust property. Elaine (wearing her trustee hat) has total control of the account, taking money out, and putting money in, as she sees fit.

The trust document states how the trust property is to be managed during Elaine's lifetime. If the trust is a Revocable Living Trust, then it will say that Elaine has the power to terminate the trust at any time and have all trust property returned to her. Should Elaine become disabled or die, then her Successor Trustee will take possession of the trust funds and manage (or distribute them) according to the directions Elaine gave in the trust document. If the trust says that once Elaine dies, the property is to be given to her beneficiary, then the Successor Trustee will do so; and in most cases without a probate procedure. If the trust directs the Successor Trustee to hold property in trust to care for a member of the Elaine's family, then the Successor Trustee will do so.

THE GOOD PART

Setting up a trust has many good features.

☆ AVOID APPOINTMENT OF CONSERVATOR

If you become disabled or too aged to handle your finances, then you do not need to worry about who takes care of your finances. Your trust appoints a Successor Trustee to take over the care of your trust if you are unable to do so. If you do not have a trust and you become incapacitated, a court may need to appoint a conservator to care for your property. The cost to establish and maintain the conservatorship is charged to you. Such legal procedures can be expensive; and once established cannot be terminated unless you die or are restored to health (NJ 3B:13A-1, 3B:13A-2, 3B:13A-5).

☆ AVOID PROBATE

In New Jersey, probate can be time consuming and very expensive. Both the Personal Representative and his attorney are entitled to payment for their services. As explained on page 142 these fees can be significant. It may be necessary to hire accountants and appraisers, as well. If you have property in two states, then two probate procedures may be necessary (one in each state) and that could be very costly. If the trust is properly drafted and your property placed into the trust, you may be able to avoid probate altogether.

☆ TAX SAVINGS:

There can be substantial Estate tax savings if you are married and you and your spouse each set up your own trust. For example, suppose you and your spouse together have an estate worth one million dollars. You can each set up your own trust with $500,000. Each trust can provide that if one of you dies, the surviving spouse can use the income from the deceased partner's trust for living expenses.

Once the second partner dies, all of the monies in the two trusts can be distributed, with no estate taxes due on either trust. By doing this, you each take advantage of your own Estate and Gift Tax Exclusion. If you don't separate the funds and one of you dies, the surviving spouse has only his own Estate and Gift Tax Exclusion. If the surviving spouse has one million dollars and the Exclusion amount $675,000, then the beneficiaries will pay taxes on anything over $675,000. If the tax rate is 37% then the beneficiaries will pay 37% of $325,000 or $120,250 in Estate taxes.

☆ PRIVACY

Your Living Trust is a private document. No one but your trustee and your beneficiaries need ever read it. If you leave property in a Will and there is a probate procedure, the Will is filed with the court. The Will becomes a public document. Anyone can go to the courthouse, read your Will and see who you did (or did not) provide for in your Will.

✰ CARE FOR A CHILD OR FAMILY MEMBER:

You can make provision in your trust to care for a child or family member after you die. If your family member is immature or a born spender, you can set up a Spendthrift Trust to protect him/her from squandering the inheritance. You can direct your Successor Trustee to use trust funds to pay for the family member's health care, education or living expenses, and nothing more.

THE PROBLEMS

With all these perks, you may be ready to call your attorney to make an appointment to set up a trust, but before doing so there are a few things you need to consider:

⌦ PROBATE MIGHT STILL BE NECESSARY

The trust only works for those items that you place in the trust. If you have property that is held jointly with another, then when you die, that property will go to the joint owner and not to the trust. If you purchase a security in your name only, and forget to put it in your trust, there will need to be a probate procedure to determine the beneficiary of that security.

☒ COST

Because of the thoroughness of the document and the fact that it is custom designed for you, a trust will cost much more to draft than a simple Will. In addition to the initial cost of the trust, it can be expensive to maintain the trust should you become disabled or die. Your Successor Trustee has the right to charge for his duties as trustee, as well as to charge for any specialized services performed.

If you choose an attorney to be Successor Trustee, the attorney has the right to charge to manage the trust, and also charge for any legal work he performs. A financial institution can charge to serve as Successor Trustee, and also charge to manage the trust portfolio. Regardless of whether you choose a professional or a family member to be Successor Trustee, you need to determine what will be charged to manage the trust.

Once you agree to the amount to be paid, you can make a provision in the trust for that amount to be paid to your Successor Trustee. If you do not make a provision for fees in your trust document, then New Jersey statute has a schedule of fees that can be charged by the Trustee. Compensation on the principal is one half of one percent (0.5%) for the first $400,000 and three tenths of one percent (0.3%) for sums over $400,000; plus 6% on income generated by trust property. Of course, a Successor Trustee who is a family member may decide to take little or no compensation (NJ 3B:18-25).

⌦ COMPLEXITY

A trust is a fairly complex document, often 20 pages long. It needs to be that long because you are establishing a vehicle for taking care of your property during your lifetime, as well as after your death. The trust usually is written in "legalese," so it may take you considerable time and effort to understand it. It is important to have your trust document prepared by an attorney who has the patience to work with you until you fully understand each paragraph of the document and are satisfied that this is what you want.

⌦ TAXES MAY STILL BE A PROBLEM:

While the Trustor is operating the trust as Trustee, all of the property held in a Revocable Living Trust is taxed as if the Trustor were holding that property in his/her own name. If the value of the trust property exceeds the Estate and Gift Tax Exclusion amount (see page 35 for the value), then unless the Trustor takes some other, more advanced, Estate Planning strategy, taxes will be due and owing once the Trustor dies.

⌦ NO CREDITOR PROTECTION

Because property held in a Revocable Living Trust is freely accessible to the Trustor, it is likewise accessible to his creditors both before and after the Trustor's death. If the Trustor dies owing money then the Personal Representative can request that trust funds can be used to pay for those debts (NJ 3B:11-1).

SPOUSE

SPOUSE'S RIGHTS IN THE TRUST

Under New Jersey law, each married partner has the right to live in the homestead i.e., their principal matrimonial residence. If you are married and wish to transfer your homestead into your trust, then your spouse must agree to the transfer and sign the deed that places the homestead into your trust. You do not need your spouse's permission to transfer real property other than your homestead into the trust; nor do you need permission from your spouse to transfer your personal property into the trust such as bank accounts and securities.

In addition to the right to live in your homestead, your spouse has the right to an ***elective share*** of your estate; i.e., your spouse has the right to inherit at least one third of all of your property. This includes property that you place into your trust. It also include gifts that you give in excess of $3,000 to any one person in the two years prior to your death.

Your spouse will not have any right to the property placed into the trust unless you make provision for your spouse as a beneficiary of the trust or unless you have neglected to make provision for the elective share; and in that case your spouse has the right to as much of the trust property as is necessary to make up the one-third elective share.

Your spouse can give up the right to live in your homestead and the right to an elective share by signing a Prenuptial or Postnuptial Agreement. (NJ 3B:8-1; 3B:8-3; 3B:8-6; 3B:8-18; 3B:28-3; 37:2-34).

THE SAFE DEPOSIT BOX

As explained on page 73, if you hold a safe deposit box in your name only, then should you die, a Personal Representative will need to be appointed in order to get possession of the contents of the box. If you have arranged your finances to avoid probate, then it is self defeating to have entry to a safe deposit box trigger a probate procedure. There are three ways to avoid the problem:

LEASE THE BOX AS TRUSTEE

One of the benefits of having a Living Trust, is that you can lease the safe deposit box in your name as Trustee. When you lease the safe deposit box you can direct the Lessor (usually a bank) that they are to allow your Successor Trustee free access to the safe deposit box in the event of your incapacity or death.

APPOINT AN AGENT

You can appoint someone to be your Agent with authority to enter the safe deposit box. You can appoint the Agent when you contract with the Lessor to rent the box; or you can have your attorney draft a Power of Attorney giving someone authority to conduct your business and to have access to your safe deposit box. Your Agent will be able to enter the box up until the time the Lessor is notified of your death (NJ 46:2B-8).

LEASE THE BOX JOINTLY WITH ANOTHER

If you are married and hold the box jointly with your spouse, then your spouse has free access to the box in the event of your death. If you are single, and do not have a Living Trust, then consider leasing the box jointly with a trusted family member. Of course, if privacy and security are important to you, then that may offset any issue of convenience for your heirs.

MAYBE PROBATE ISN'T ALL THAT BAD

If you hold all of your property in trust or jointly with another, you may be able to avoid probate and have your property go directly to your heirs, but you may have reason not to choose either of these methods. Maybe you don't have money at this time to pay an attorney to set up a trust. Maybe you do not want to hold your money jointly with anyone because you are concerned about losing your independence or maybe you are concerned about keeping your money secure.

If you arrange all of your finances so that the money goes directly to a few beneficiaries, then this plan may not be as flexible as you wish. This is especially the case if you wish to give gifts to several charities or to minor children instead of just one or two beneficiaries. For example, if you hold all of your property so that it goes directly to your child without the need for probate, then your child becomes the legal owner of your property as of your date of death. If you tell your child to use some of that money as a donation to your church and some of it for your grandchild's education, then that puts an unreasonable burden on your child because you were not specific as to exactly how much of that money you wished to be donated. Also you did not say how the money is to be used for the child. Is the money for tuition only? Can the money be used to pay the child's living expenses?

Even if you give your child specific instructions about how the money is to be spent, and even if your child is honorable and with the best intentions, it may be that your grandchild gets none of the money, because your child is sued or falls upon hard times and is forced to use that money to pay debts. If you keep your property in your own name and leave a Will giving a certain amount of money for your grandchild, then he/she will know exactly how much money you left and the purpose of that gift.

Many people decide that the Will is the best route to go but do not act upon it, thinking it unnecessary to prepare a Will until they are very old and about to die. But according to reports published by the National Center for Health Statistics (a division of the U.S. Department of Health and Human Services) 2 of every 10 people who die in any given year are under the age of 60. Twenty percent may seem like a small number until it hits close to home as it did with a young couple. The couple was having difficulty conceiving a child. They went from doctor to doctor until they met someone just beginning his practice. With his knowledge of the latest advances in medicine, he was able to help them. The birth of their child was a moment of joy and gratitude. They asked a nurse to take a picture of them all together — the happy couple, the newborn child and the doctor who made it all happen. Happiness radiated from the picture, but one of them would be dead within six months.

You might think it was the child. An infant's life is so fragile. SIDS and all manner of childhood diseases can threaten a little one. But no, he grew up to be a healthy young man.

If you looked at the picture, you might guess the husband. Overweight and stressed out; his ruddy complexion suggested high blood pressure. He looked like a typical heart- attack-prone type A personality.
No, he was fine and went on to enjoy raising his son.

Probably the wife. She had such a difficult time with the pregnancy and the delivery was especially hard. Perhaps it was all too much for her.
No, she recovered and later had two more children.

It was the doctor who was killed in a three car collision.

Though we all agree, that one never knows, still people put off making a Will figuring that if they die before getting around to it, New Jersey law will take over and their property will be distributed in the manner that they would have wanted anyway. The problem with that logic is the complexity of the Laws of Intestate Succession. If you are survived by a spouse, child, parent or sibling, then it isn't too difficult to figure out who will inherit your property. But if none of these survive you, the ultimate beneficiary of your property may not be the person you would have chosen, had you taken the time to do so.

An important reason to make a Will is so that you can choose your Personal Representative and come to an understanding about how much compensation he/she is to receive. You can state that value in your Will. Unless there is some problem with the probate causing significant extra work for your Representative, this is the amount that will be paid (NJ 3B:18-3).

Another benefit to making a Will is that you can make provision for who will get your personal property, including your car. If you make a gift of your car in your Will, then it will be relatively simple for your car to be transferred to the beneficiary. If you do not make a specific gift of your car in your Will, then it becomes part of your Probate Estate. Your Personal Representative will decide what to do with the car. He can sell it and include the proceeds of the sale in the estate funds to be distributed to your residuary beneficiaries; or he can give the car to one of the beneficiary of your estate as part of that beneficiary's share of the estate. Without a Will, your Personal Representative gets to make these decisions. With a Will you can decide who is to inherit each item of your estate. You can even provide for the care of your pet as these next few pages will show.

FOR PET LOVERS

A woman died at peace,
leaving her fortune
and care of her cat to her niece.
Alas, the fortune and the cat
Soon disappeared after that.

You could make provision in your Will for the care of your pet, but the moral of the above limerick, is that leaving your money to someone to do the job may not be the best route to go.

LAWYER TRUST FOR CARE OF PET

If you are serious about caring for your pet after your death, you can employ an attorney to set up a separate trust for the care of your pet, or you can have the attorney include a trust provision in your Will.

The trust document will direct the trustee to pay sufficient monies to a custodian for the care of the pet. You also need to name a beneficiary (a person or charitable organization) to receive whatever may remain in the trust after the pet dies.

If you intend the trustee to also serve as custodian of the pet, then you can ask the beneficiary to regularly check on the pet to see to it that the pet is treated humanely, if not benevolently.

CARE OF PETS (Continued)

If you don't have the resources to set up a trust to care for your pet, you can still ask a fellow pet lover to care for the animal. If no one among your circle of family and friends is able to do so, then ask your pet's veterinarian to consider starting an "Orphaned Pet Service" to assist in finding new homes for pets who lose their owners. It is good public relations and a potential source of income. If this is agreeable to Veterinarian, you can make arrangements in your Will to pay the Vet to care for the pet until a suitable family can be found. This is a more humane approach than the, all too common practice, of putting a pet "to sleep" rather than have the pet suffer the loss of its master. And in at least one case, that reasoning backfired.

Eleanor always had a pet in the house. After her husband died, her two poodles were her constant companions. When Eleanor became ill with cancer, she worried about what would happen to her "buddies" if she died. She finally decided it best to have her family put them to sleep when she died.

Eleanor endured surgery, chemotherapy, radiation therapy, and even some holistic remedies, but she continued to go downhill. Eleanor's family came in to visit her at the hospital to say their last good-byes. She was so ill, she didn't even recognize them. No one thought she could last the day. Because the family was from out of state, and time short, they decided to put the pets to sleep so they need only take care of the funeral arrangements when she died.

To everyone's surprise, Eleanor rallied. She lived two more long, lonely years. She often said she wished they had put her to sleep instead of her buddies.

PROVIDING FOR THE MINOR CHILD

Parents have a special responsibility. They need to make provision for the care of their child in the event they both die or become incapacitated before the child is grown. It is unusual for a child to lose both parents, but it does happen, and parents need to provide for this possibility.

CARING FOR THE PERSON OF THE CHILD

A child must be cared for in two ways, the ***person*** of the child and the ***estate*** (the property) of the child. To care for the person of the child, someone must be in charge of the child's everyday living, not only food and shelter but to provide social, ethical and religious training. Someone must have legal authority to make medical decisions and see to the child's education.

To care for the child's estate, someone must take charge of monies left to the child. That person is responsible to see that the monies are used for the care of the child and that anything left over is preserved until the child becomes an adult.

If one parent dies, then it is the right, and duty, of the surviving parent to care for the child. But it could happen that both parents become incapacitated or die before the child is grown. In New Jersey, parents have the right to appoint someone to care for their child in the event that neither of them are able to do so. Such appointment is explained on the next page.

THE TEMPORARY GUARDIAN

New Jersey law allows parents to appoint someone to take over any of the parents powers regarding the care, custody or property of a minor — with the exception of giving that person the right to consent to the marriage of the minor or to consent to the adoption of the minor. The appointment is done by means of a Power of Attorney and it cannot be for a period greater than six months (NJ 3B:12-39). This appointment is appropriate should the parent need to be absent from the child for a short period of time. The Power of Attorney needs to be drafted by an attorney. If the parent has limited funds then the parent can seek the assistance of Legal Aid.

THE STANDBY GUARDIAN

It may happen that a parent who has sole custody of a child becomes seriously ill and in jeopardy of not being able to care for the child. Under such circumstance the parent can appoint a ***Standby Guardian*** to care for the child in the event of the parent's incapacity or death. New Jersey statute 3B:12-74 contains a form that the parent can use to make the appointment. The parent can obtain the form by looking up the statute at any law library or from the Internet (see page xii).

In the event of the parent's incapacity or death, the standby guardian can immediately take over the care of the child. Within 60 days, the Standby Guardian must petition (ask) the Surrogate's Court in the county of the child's residence to be appointed as the child's legal guardian (NJ 3B:12-73, 3B:12-12).

Either parent has the right to name someone in their Will to be the guardian of their child in the event that the parent dies before the child is grown, and the other parent is unable to care for the child. It would be nice if both parents name the same person in their respective Wills to be guardian, but the reality is that parents often disagree about who is best qualified to raise the child. New Jersey law provides that if one parent dies, the other parent can either assume responsibility for the care of the child or the surviving parent can agree to the appointment of the guardian chosen by the deceased parent (NJ 3B:12-13, 3B:12-14, 3B:12-15).

If you have sole custody of your child, then person you name to be Guardian can assume the care of the child upon your death, but that person needs to be appointed as the child's legal Guardian by the Surrogate's court. In appointing a Guardian, the judge's primary concern is the best interests of the child. If the child is over the age of 14, the judge will give priority to the person preferred by the child. If the child is under 14, the judge will give priority to the person you chose as Guardian, but if the judge determines that person is not qualified to be Guardian, he will appoint someone who is (NJ 3B:12-12).

LEAVING PROPERTY FOR THE CHILD

As any parent is well aware, it is expensive to raise a child. People that you might consider to be the best choice to serve as your child's Guardian might not be able to do so unless you leave sufficient monies to pay for the care of the child. If you are a person of limited finances, then consider purchasing a term life insurance policy on your life and/or on the life of the other parent of the child. If you can only afford one policy, then insure the life of the parent who contributes most to the support of the child.

Term insurance policies are relatively inexpensive if you limit the term to just that period of time until your child becomes an adult. Some companies offer a combination of term life and disability insurance. As with any other purchase, it is important to comparison shop to obtain the best price for the coverage.

If you are married to the parent of your child, then the beneficiary of the term insurance policy can be your spouse with your child as an alternate beneficiary. Married or single, you can name your child as the primary beneficiary of the policy. For policies over $5,000, the court will appoint a guardian of the child's estate — usually the child's surviving parent. Guardianship procedures can be expensive, so consider appointing a Custodian of the insurance proceeds (see page 174).

☎ LAWYER A TRUST FOR THE CHILD

If you have sufficient monies to care for your child until adulthood, then consult with an attorney about setting up a trust for the child or drafting a Will with a trust provision in the event you die before the child is grown. The only problem with having a trust included in your Will is that the trust is funded by your Probate Estate; and as such may increase the cost of probate as well as the cost of administering the trust. If you have a significant amount of money, the better route might be to set up a Revocable Living Trust. You can fund the trust while you are alive and bypass probate altogether.

The person you name as Trustee will handle the trust funds should you die before the child reaches maturity. You can name the other parent as your Trustee, or if you wish, you can appoint a financial institution to manage the trust funds. If you do not appoint the other parent as Trustee, then that parent still has the right, and duty, to care for the child. If you instruct the Trustee to use trust funds for the child's support and maintenance, then the Trustee can set up a payment schedule with the child's parent to use the funds for everyday necessities.

If you instruct the Trustee to keep all of the funds invested until the child reaches maturity, then the Trustee will do so and distribute the trust funds directly to the child at whatever age you specify in the trust document.

PROVIDING FOR THE STEPCHILD

Perhaps the reason that the story of Cinderella has such universal appeal is that many stepchildren, at one point or another, feel left out. The law seems to reinforce that perception. Should your spouse die, then you, and not your stepchild, have the authority to agree to an anatomical gift (NJ 26:6-58). If all of you spouse's property is held jointly with you, then should your spouse die first, your stepchild will be left nothing.

Of course giving you the right to inherit all of your spouse's estate must be a decision that is agreeable to your spouse. If your spouse wants your step-child to inherit property, then your spouse can arrange his/her finances so that the child will inherit property. Hopefully, your spouse will consult with an estate planning attorney who can explain the best way to achieve that goal, else that intent could be thwarted and the child end up with less than your spouse intended as was the case in the example given on page 116.

Similarly, if your spouse wants his/her child to have authority to make the parent's medical decisions or handle the parent's finances should the parent become incapacitated, then your spouse can give his/her child that authority by signing an Advance Health Care Directive and a Power of Attorney.

It isn't just stepchildren who can be left out if no provision is made. Even children from a long-standing marriage can be cut off against the wishes of a parent. A parent may assume that all of their children will be treated equally once they are both gone, but consider that the last to die is the one who gets to decide "who gets what." That was the case with Joan and Herbert. They were a devoted couple, married over forty years. Herb was the breadwinner, but he was content to let Joan handle all of the finances.

Joan wanted to be sure that each of their three daughters would always have a decent place to live. They purchased a three story house and each of the daughters moved into a different floor of the home. It was the parent's intent that once they were both gone, the daughters would inherit and occupy the building.

The couple held everything jointly. When Joan died, all of their property, including the home, was owned by Herbert. The grief suffered by Herbert at his wife's passing was more than he could bear. He alternated between sadness, despair and anger.

His middle daughter took the brunt of his anger. Their relationship had always been strained. She felt she could never live up to her father's expectations. She was not the cute baby of the family as was her younger sister. She was not the eldest daughter who always seemed to make her Dad proud. He always made her feel that she was a disappointment to him. Once her mother died, she had no one left to buffer the relationship with her father.

Soon after Joan's death, Herbert had an attorney draft a Will leaving all to his eldest and youngest daughter. None of the children knew what he had done.

Herbert decided to take a trip to Europe to try to escape the pain of his mourning. When he was in France, he suffered a heart attack and died. He died within 6 months of Joan's death.

If he had returned from Europe, Herbert may have reconciled with his daughter, but as it happened, there was no time for them to develop a better relationship.

With both their parents gone, the eldest and youngest daughter decided to sell the home. The youngest sister offered some of the proceeds to middle daughter. The middle daughter refused the offer with unkind words. Being offered less than her one-third share, meant to her that her sisters approved of their father's action. It was as if she were being disinherited all over again.

It was unfortunate that Joan's best plans were thwarted. They didn't have to be. She and Herbert could have kept a life estate in the property with the remainder going to all three girls. That would have ensured that each daughter received an equal inheritance. More importantly, the family would not have been torn by the hurt and anger that was more a product of a husband's grief rather than the absence of a father's love.

PROVIDING FOR INCAPACITY

As the life expectancy of the population increases, so does the percentage of the population who suffer from debilitating diseases such as Alzheimer's and Parkinsons'. As a person ages, his chances for suffering dementia as a result of a stroke or other diseases increases. It is estimated that more than 50% of the population who are 85 or older, suffer from some degree of dementia.

If you are concerned that you may become disabled in the future, you need to consider who will care for your property and who will take care of your person. You can have an attorney prepare a trust. You can be trustee of the funds while you have capacity. Once you can no longer do so, then the person you name as Successor Trustee will take over.

If you do not have sufficient assets to justify the cost of employing an attorney to draft a trust, you can appoint someone to be your Agent to care for your property by signing a Power of Attorney; and you can appoint a Health Care Representative to make your medical decisions by signing an Advance Directive for Health Care.

☎ LAWYER

A SPECIAL NEEDS TRUST FOR THE INCAPACITATED

If a person is incapacitated, both the federal and state government provide assistance with programs such as social security disability benefits and custodial nursing home care under the Medicaid program. The family often supplements the government program by providing for the incapacitated person's ***special needs,*** such as clothing, hobbies, special education, outings to a movie or a sports event — things that give the incapacitated person some quality of life.

To be eligible for government assistance programs the incapacitated must be essentially without funds. Caretakers fear that leaving money to the incapacitated in a will or trust will disqualify the incapacitated from further government assistance. Understanding this dilemma, the federal government allows caretakers to set up a ***Special Needs*** trust with the incapacitated as the beneficiary of the trust. One type of Special Needs Trust is the ***Disability Trust*** as authorized by 42 U.S.C. 1382c(a)(3). A trustee is appointed to use trust funds to provide for the special needs of the incapacitated. If any trust funds are left after the incapacitated dies, then those funds must be used to reimburse the state for monies spent on behalf of the incapacitated person.

There are other types of special needs trusts that are allowed under the law. An experienced Elder Law attorney can explain the different options available and assist the family member in preparing a Will or trust that will provide for the incapacitated person's special needs once the family member dies.

☎ LAWYER

PROVIDING FOR THE CARETAKER

If you are the caretaker or the court appointed Conservator of someone who is incapacitated, then in addition to preparing your own estate plan, you need to be concerned about who will care for the incapacitated person should something happen to you. Someone will need to make medical decisions for the incapacitated person and see to it that he/she is properly housed and fed.

APPOINTMENT OF A SUCCESSOR CARETAKER

Often a family member will agree to take responsibility for the care of an incapacitated person in the event that the caretaker dies. But perhaps no one wants the job, or the opposite case, too many want to have control. For example, if a parent is incapacitated, one child may want the parent to remain at home with the assistance of a home health care worker. Another child may think the best place for the parent is an assisted living facility with 24 hour care. The caretaker spouse may be concerned that a tug-of-war will erupt once he dies.

In such case, the caretaker should consult with an attorney to ensure future care for the incapacitated person. The attorney may suggest establishing a trust or having a Conservator appointed for the incapacitated person while the parent/caretaker is alive. Once the Conservatorship is in place, the court will continue to supervise the care of the incapacitated person until he/she is restored to health or dies.

ARRANGING TO PAY BILLS

When people draft a Will they are more concerned about giving their possessions away than they are about taking into account what they actually have to give. This was the case with Larry. He had no family to speak of. After his wife died, he bought a condominium in Springfield. Over the years, he developed a close network of friends. They became his family. Larry did not have much money. He had a mortgage on the condominium. His car was leased. He wanted his friends to know how much they meant to him so he had a Will drafted giving all he owned to five close friends.

The friends appreciated the gesture but the probate procedure turned out to be a nightmare. They had to keep current the mortgage payments and the maintenance fees until the condominium was sold. Because Larry left little cash, this money had to come out of the beneficiaries' pockets. Two were living on their social security income and they had to borrow money from the others to contribute to their share of the upkeep.

The beneficiaries had no money to settle the lease on the car. Even if they did, they decided that there was no point in doing so because the amount needed to obtain clear title was greater than the current market value of the car. The beneficiaries decided not to make any further payment and they returned the car to the leasing agent. Their decision turned out to be a losing proposition. The leasing agent took the car, sold it and then sued the estate for the balance of the monies owed on the lease.

Because the beneficiaries had to quickly liquidate the estate, the condominium sold for less than it would have had they the time, energy and resources to fix it up. After they settled with the leasing agent, paid off the funeral expenses, mortgage, and probate fees there was only a few hundred dollars left. That was a lot of work and stress for nothing.

The pity was that Larry could have arranged his finances so that his beneficiaries were not burdened by his debt. He could have taken out mortgage insurance as part of the loan package. In most cases the cost of the insurance is nominal and is included as part of the monthly mortgage payment.

Larry could have done the same when he leased the car. Most leasing contracts offer term life insurance as an option. The cost of such insurance depends on the age of the person, the term of the loan and the amount of monies owed, but the premium paid each month is just a small fraction of the loan payment.

Even if Larry just arranged for payment of one of these debts, his beneficiaries would have come away with the gift that Larry intended, instead of the headache that they inherited.

PROVIDE FOR CREDIT CARD DEBT

If you have significant credit card debt, you need to consider how that debt will be paid once you die. Most credit card companies offer insurance policies and include the premium as part of your monthly payment. If you have such insurance, then should you die, any outstanding balance is paid. It benefits the credit card company to offer life insurance as part of the credit package, because they are assured of prompt payment should the borrower die. However, if you have little or no assets and no one other than yourself is liable to pay the debt, you may have no incentive to pay for insurance that can only benefit the lender.

As discussed in Chapters 2 and 4, if you hold a credit card jointly with another person, both of you are equally liable to pay the debt. If one of you dies, the other is responsible to pay the bill regardless of who ran up the bill. If paying that bill could be a struggle for the surviving debtor, then the better route to go is for each of you to have your own credit card.

Still another reason not to hold a joint credit card is that each of you can establish your own line of credit. This is especially important if you are married and one of you is retired or has been out of the job market for any period of time. Should the breadwinner die, it may be difficult for the surviving partner to establish credit if he/she has no recent work record It is easier for the unemployed spouse to establish a line of credit when he/she is married to someone who is working.

The good part of purchasing loan insurance — be it credit card insurance, mortgage insurance or car insurance, is that you can usually purchase the insurance without taking a medical examination. The down side is that such insurance may be more expensive than a life insurance policy. If you are in fairly good health, consider taking out a life insurance policy to cover all of your outstanding loans. The cost of the single life insurance policy may be significantly less than purchasing separate loan insurance policies.

The estate planning strategy of purchasing life insurance to pay off all of your loans works best if you are married and your spouse is jointly liable for your debts. If you name your spouse as beneficiary of the life insurance policy, then he/she can use the life insurance funds to pay off all monies owed. If you name your spouse, child or dependent relative and that person has no legal obligation to pay your debts, and if your primary residence is in the State of New Jersey, none of your creditors can force your beneficiary to use any part of those funds to pay your debts (NJ 17B:24-6).

If you want the insurance funds used to pay your debts, then this may not be the way to go. But, if you want to be sure that someone receives money for their care after you are gone, and you do not want those funds reduced by the cost of probate or to pay off your debts, then this strategy should accomplish your goal. Which brings us to the issue of life insurance — should you have it? How much is enough? The answer to these questions depends on the "sleep at night" factor, namely how much insurance do you need to make you not worry about insurance coverage when you go to sleep at night? It is often more an emotional than a financial issue.

Some people have an "every man for himself" attitude and are content to have no life insurance at all. Others worry about how their loved ones will manage if they are not around to support them. The same person may have different thoughts about insurance coverage as the circumstances of their life changes — from no coverage in their bachelor days to more-than-enough coverage in their child rearing days to just-enough-to-bury-me in their senior years. Insurance companies recognize that people's needs change over the years. Many companies offer flexible insurance coverage. As with any consumer item, it is a good idea to shop around.

HEALTH CARE INSURANCE

The pharmacology industry is well motivated to produce drugs that manage the ills associated with aging. Their research has led to a wealth of pharmacological remedies that do not cure, but do allow people to live relatively comfortably into advanced age. The only problem is the cost of these drugs. Medicare covers the treatment of life-threatening brushes with heart disease, stroke, cancer and diabetes; but, as of this writing, Medicare does not pay for maintenance medication that is often necessary once the condition is stabilized.

Medicare is also limited in long term health care coverage. It does not pay for extended nursing care. Medicare pays for the first 20 days of skilled nursing care. Medicare pays $95.50 for days 21 through 100. After 100 days, you are on your own. A nursing home stay of one or two years can wipe out the life savings of most working people. Once savings are gone, the government provides care in the form of Medicaid coverage.

Your best estate plan could be sabotaged by a lengthy, or debilitating illness. If you are poor, long-term nursing care may not be of concern to you, because all your needs should be covered under Medicaid. If you are very wealthy, you may not worry because you have more than enough money to pay for your care. But the rest of us need to think about ways to provide for long-term health care.

For those concerned about the loss of life savings because of illness, there is supplemental and/or long-term health care insurance. There are many different insurance plans available. You can call the National Association of Insurance Commissioners at (816) 842-3600 and they will forward to you, free of charge, the publication:

A SHOPPER'S GUIDE TO LONG TERM CARE INSURANCE

If you have a specific question about long term care insurance, then you can call the New Jersey Department of Community Affairs, Division on Aging at (800) 792-8820 for further information.

As with any health care insurance coverage, cost is a major factor. Many cannot afford the cost of the insurance premium. Others are not insurable because of a pre-existing condition. If such is the case with you, then consider consulting with an experienced financial planner and/or an experienced Elder Law attorney. They can suggest different ways to protect and preserve your life savings in the event that you require long term health care.

ANNUITIES TO SPREAD THE INHERITANCE

Most beneficiaries go through their inheritance within two years. For many, the reason the money is gone so soon, is that there just wasn't much money to inherit in the first place. But for others, it's a spending frenzy.

People's spending habits remain much the same throughout their lifetime. Some people are squirrels, always saving for the winter. For others, it's:

Earn-A-Penny Spend-A-Penny

Most of us fall somewhere in between. We are not extravagant in our spending habits, yet it is a struggle to save. But why should we struggle to purchase an insurance policy if the intended beneficiary will spend it in a few months?

If you want to leave an insurance policy benefit to someone you love, but the intended beneficiary is immature, or a born spendthrift, then a simple solution to the problem may be to purchase an annuity rather than life insurance.

An annuity is a type of insurance policy that can be set up so that your beneficiary (the ***annuitant***) receives money on a monthly, or yearly basis, rather than a single lump sum payment when you die. There are different kinds of annuities, so again, it is important to shop around.

LAWYER

PROVIDING FOR THE FAMILY BUSINESS

If you are the sole proprietor of a business, then you need to give considerable thought to what will happen to that business in the event of your incapacity or death. Can the business to continue operate without you? Is it your intent that whoever inherits your business take over its daily operations or do you think it best to have the business sold and have the proceeds of the sale given to your beneficiary?

If you do not make provision for the orderly transfer of your business, then a court may need to make that decision for you. In particular, if you are declared incapacitated then your court appointed guardian will need court approval to continue the business. If you die, then your Personal Representative may need to decide what to do with the business.

In addition to the running of the business you need to consider how company debts will be paid. If your business is highly leveraged (business talk for "owe lots of money"), then you also need to consider how those loans will be paid, should you be unable to continue operating the business. We have already discussed key man insurance as a means of providing funds to the company. An attorney who is experienced in business law (commercial law, corporation, banking, bankruptcy, franchise law, etc.) can offer other suggestions as to the best method of ensuring that the business continues its operation, or terminates in an orderly fashion — whichever is applicable in your case.

SMALL GIFTS MATTER

Many who have lost someone close report that the distribution of the personal property caused the greatest conflict. If there is no need for a probate procedure and the decedent died without a Will, then the next of kin need to decide, among themselves, how personal property is to be distributed. Without guidance from the decedent and no Personal Representative with authority to make decisions, there could be much disagreement and hard feelings, as was the case in the example given on page 123.

Under New Jersey law, this is easily avoided. Whether you have a Will or not, you have the right to make a list of your personal property and indicate who is to receive each item on the list. It does not need to be a formal document. It does not need to be witnessed. All you need to do is describe each item so that it is easily identified; name the beneficiary of the item and then sign the writing (NJ 3B:3-11).

If you have a Will, you can attach the list to your Will and your Personal Representative will distribute your personal property according to your directions.

You should not use the list to make money gifts, nor is it advisable to make gifts of expensive items, such as a valuable painting, or a gift of your car. Items of significant value should be included in your Will or Trust. The separate writing is best used to distribute gifts that have more sentimental, than monetary value.

Joint Ownership?
A POD Account?
A TOD Security?
A Trust?
A Will?
An Insurance Policy???

This chapter offers so many options that the reader may be more confused than when he was blissfully unenlightened.

As with most things in life, you may find there are no ultimate solutions, just alternatives. The right choice for you is the one that best accomplishes your goal. This being the case, you first need to determine what you want to accomplish with the money that you leave. Think about what will happen to your property if you were to die suddenly, without making any plan different from the one you now have.

Who will get your property?
Will there be any estate tax?
Will they need to go through probate?

If the answers to these questions are not what you wish, then you need to work to retitle your property to accomplish your goals. For those with significant assets, — especially those with estates large enough to pay estate taxes, a trip to an experienced Estate Planning attorney may be well worth the consultation fee.

YOUR ESTATE PLAN RECORD

Once you are satisfied with your estate plan, then the final thing to consider is whether your heirs will be able to locate your assets once you are deceased.

Most people have their business records in one place, their Will in another place, car titles and deeds in still another place. When someone dies, their beneficiaries may feel as if they are playing a game of "hide and seek" with the decedent. The game might be fun if it were not for the fact that things not found may be forever lost. For example, suppose you die in an accident and no one knows you are insured by your credit card company for accidental death in the amount of $25,000. The only one to profit is the insurance company, which is just that much richer because no one told them that you died as a result of an accident.

How about a key to a safe deposit box located in another state? Will anyone find it? Even if they find the key, how will they find the box?

It is not difficult to arrange things so that your affairs are always in order. It amounts to being aware of what you own (and owe) and keeping a record of your possessions. A side benefit is that by doing so, you will always know where all your business records are. If you ever spent time trying to collect information to file your taxes or trying to find a lost stock or bond certificate, you will appreciate the value of organizing your records.

Heirs need all the help they can get. It is difficult enough dealing with the loss, without the frustration of trying to locate important documents. Your heirs will have no problem locating your assets if you keep all of your records in a single place. It can be a desk drawer or a file cabinet or even a shoe box. It is helpful if you keep a separate file or folder for each type of investment. You might consider setting up the following folders:

THE BANK & SECURITIES FOLDER

Store your original certificates for stocks, bonds, mutual funds, certificates of deposit, in a folder labeled BANK & SECURITIES FOLDER. In addition to the original certificate include a copy of the contract you signed with each financial institution. The contract will show where you have funds and who you named as beneficiary or joint owner of the account. If someone owes you money and has signed a Promissory note or mortgage that identifies you as the lender, then you can store these documents in this folder as well.

If you wish to store your original documents in a safe deposit box, then keep a record of the location of the safe deposit box, and the number of the box, in this folder. Make a copy of all of the items stored in the box and place the copies in this folder. If you have an extra key to the box, then put the key in the folder. If you are the only person with access to the box, it may take a probate procedure to remove items from the box once you die. Consider allowing someone you trust to be able to gain entry to the box in the event of your incapacity or death.

THE LIABILITY FOLDER

The LIABILITY FOLDER should contain all loan documents of debts that you owe. For example, if you purchased real property and have a mortgage on that property, then put a copy of the mortgage and promissory note in this folder. If you owe money on a car, put the promissory note and chattel mortgage on the car in the file. If you have a credit card, put a copy of the contract you signed with the credit card company in this file.

Many people never take the time to calculate their ***net worth*** (what a person owns less what that person owes). By having a record of your assets and outstanding debts, you can calculate your net worth whenever you wish.

THE INSURANCE/PENSION FOLDER

The INSURANCE FOLDER is for each original insurance policy that you own, be it car insurance, homeowner's insurance or a health care insurance policy. If you purchased real property, you probably received a title commitment at closing and the original title insurance policy some weeks later when you received your original deed from recording. If you cannot locate the title insurance policy, then contact the closing agent and have them send you a copy of your title policy. If you have a pension or an annuity, then include those documents in this folder as well.

THE DEED FOLDER

Many people save every scrap of paper associated with the closing of real property. If you closed recently on real estate and there was a mortgage involved in the purchase, you probably walked away from closing with enough paper to wallpaper your kitchen. If you wish, you can keep all of those papers in a separate file that identifies the property, for example:

CLOSING PAPERS FOR THE OCEAN CITY PROPERTY.

Set aside the original deed (or a copy if the original is in a safe deposit box) and place it into a separate DEED FOLDER. Include deeds to parcels of real property, cemetery deeds, condominium deeds, cooperative shares to real property, timesharing certificates, etc. Include deeds to out of state property as well as New Jersey property in the DEED FOLDER. If you have a mortgage on your property, then put a copy of the mortgage and promissory note in a separate LIABILITY FOLDER.

THE TAX RECORD FOLDER

Your Personal Representative (or next of kin) will need to file your final income tax returns. Keep a copy of your tax returns (both federal and state) for the past three years in your Tax Record Folder.

THE PERSONAL PROPERTY FOLDER

MOTOR VEHICLES

Put all motor vehicle titles in a Personal Property folder. This includes cars, mobile homes, boats, planes, etc. If you owe money on the vehicle, the lender may have possession of the title certificate. If such is the case, then put a copy of the title certificate and registration in this folder and a copy of the promissory note or chattel mortgage in a separate liability folder.

If you have a boat or plane, then identify the location of the motor vehicle. For example, if you are leasing space in an airplane hanger or in a marina, keep a copy of the leasing agreement in this file.

JEWELRY

If you own expensive jewelry, keep a picture of the item together with the sales receipt or written appraisal in this folder.

COLLECTOR'S ITEMS

If you own a valuable art collection, or a coin collection or any other item of significant value, include a picture of the item in this file. Also include evidence of ownership of the item, such as a sales receipt or a certificate of authenticity, or a written appraisal of the property.

THE PERSONAL RECORD FOLDER

The PERSONAL RECORD FOLDER should include documents that relate to you personally, such as a birth certificate, naturalization papers, pre-nuptial or post- nuptial agreement, Will or Trust Agreement, marriage certificate, divorce papers, army records, social security card; etc. If you have an Advance Directive for Health Care, or Power of Attorney, then this is a good place for these documents. If you placed the original document in a safe deposit box, then keep a copy in this folder together with the location of the original.

FOR FEDERAL RETIREES

If you are a Federal Retiree, you should have received your **P**ERSONAL **I**DENTIFICATION **N**UMBER (**PIN**) and the person who will inherit your pension (your ***survivor annuitant***) should have received his/her own PIN as well. It is relatively simple to obtain this during your lifetime, but it may be difficult and/or stressful for your survivor annuitant to work through the system once you are gone. To get information on obtaining these numbers you can call the RETIREMENT INFORMATION OFFICE at (888) 767-6738. For the hearing impaired, call (800) 878-5707.

Upon your death, your survivor annuitant may be entitled to death benefits. These benefits are not automatic. Your survivor annuitant must apply for them by submitting a death claim to the Office of Personnel Management. Your survivor needs to know that it is necessary to apply and also how to apply. See page 30 for an explanation about how to apply for benefits and then make that information available to your family.

THE *If I Die* FILE

In addition to keeping your up-to-date records in a single place, you need to let your family know the location of these items. You can set up an ***If I Die*** file and make that file accessible to someone you trust or to the person you appointed as Personal Representative in your Will; i.e., let that person know the location of the file and how to get it in the event of your death.

You can use the form on the next page as a basis for the information to include in the file.

If I Die

then the following information will help settle my estate:

INFORMATION FOR DEATH CERTIFICATE

MY FULL LEGAL NAME ____________________

MY SOCIAL SECURITY NO. ____________________

MY USUAL OCCUPATION ____________________

BIRTH DATE AND BIRTH PLACE ____________________

If naturalized, date & place ____________________

MY FATHER'S NAME ____________________

MY MOTHER'S MAIDEN NAME ____________________

PERSONS TO BE NOTIFIED OF MY DEATH

____

____

____

FUNERAL AND BURIAL ARRANGEMENTS

LOCATION OF BURIAL SITE

____

LOCATION OF PRENEED FUNERAL CONTRACT

____

FOR VETERAN or SPOUSE BURIAL IN A NATIONAL CEMETERY

BRANCH____________________SERIAL NO.____________________

VETERAN'S RANK ____________________

VETERAN'S VA CLAIM NUMBER ____________________

DATE AND PLACE OF ENTRY INTO SERVICE:

____

DATE AND PLACE OF SEPARATION FROM SERVICE:

____

LOCATION OF OFFICIAL MILITARY DISCHARGE
OR DD 214 FORM____________________

LOCATION OF LEGAL DOCUMENTS

BIRTH CERTIFICATE ______________________________

MARRIAGE CERTIFICATE______________________________

DIVORCE DECREE ______________________________

PASSPORT ______________________________

WILL OR TRUST ______________________________

DEEDS ______________________________

MORTGAGES ______________________________

TITLE TO MOTOR VEHICLES ______________________________

HEALTH CARE DIRECTIVES ______________________________

NAME, PHONE NO. OF ATTORNEY______________________________

LOCATION OF FINANCIAL RECORDS

INSURANCE POLICIES:

NAME OF COMPANY & PHONE NO. ______________________________

LOCATION OF POLICY ______________________________

BENEFICIARY OF POLICY ______________________________

PENSIONS/ANNUITIES:

IF FEDERAL RETIREE: PIN NUMBER: ______________________________

NAME OF SURVIVOR ______________________________

SURVIVOR PIN NUMBER ______________________________

BANK

BANK: ACCOUNT NO.______________________________

NAME, ADDRESS OF FINANCIAL INSTITUTION

____

LOCATION OF SAFE DEPOSIT BOX ______________________________

LOCATION OF KEY TO BOX ______________________________

SECURITIES

NAME AND PHONE NUMBER OF BROKER

____

TAX RECORDS FOR PAST 3 YEARS

LOCATION______________________________

ACCOUNTANT: NAME, PHONE # ______________________________

____

WHEN TO UPDATE YOUR ESTATE PLAN

We discussed people's natural disinclination to make an estate plan until they are faced with their own mortality. Many believe that they will make just one Will and then die (maybe that's why they put off making a Will). The reality is, most people who make a Will change it at least once before they die.

If you have an estate plan, it is important to update it when any of the following events take place:

✍ RELOCATION TO A NEW STATE OR COUNTRY

If you move within state there is no need to change your estate plan, but if you move to another state or country, you need to check to see whether your plan is valid in that state. Each state (and country) has its own laws relating to the inheritance of property and those laws are very different from each other. Items that are protected from a creditor in one state, may not be creditor proof in another state. Each state has its own estate tax structure. If estate taxes are high, you may need an estate plan that will minimize the impact of those taxes.

Each state has its own, unique, laws of intestate succession. Who has the right to inherit your property in one state may be different from who can inherit your property in another. The rights of a spouse in a community property state are very different from those in other states. If you have a Will, then you need to determine whether your Will is valid in the new state. If you move to another state or country, it is important to either educate yourself about the laws of the state, or to consult with an attorney who can assist you in reviewing your estate plan to see if that plan will accomplish your goals in that state.

✍ A SIGNIFICANT CHANGE IN THE LAW

It is important to keep up with changes in the law. You can do so by reading your daily newspaper, listening to the news on television, and/or keeping in touch with your attorney to learn if any new law will affect your estate plan. One change currently under discussion is to do away with the Federal Estate Tax. If that happens, then you may want to determine how this impacts your current estate plan. It is a good idea to discuss any significant change in the law with your attorney.

✍ A CHANGE IN RELATIONSHIP

If you get married, divorced, have a child, or a beneficiary of your estate dies, then you should examine your estate plan to determine whether it needs to be revised. If your marriage is annulled or you are divorced, there are certain changes that take place by law. For example, if you divorce and then die before you get around to changing your Will (or Trust), then any provision that you made for your ex-spouse in the Will or Trust will be read as if your ex-spouse died before you (NJ 3B:3-14).

But it is important to not just rely on the law. Best to change all documents after the divorce or separation. That includes your Advance Directive for Health Care, Power of Attorney, deeds, etc. You should also change the beneficiary of your insurance policies, pension plans, etc.

GAMES DECEDENTS PLAY

We discussed the game of "hide and seek" some decedents play with their heirs. A variation of that game is the "wild goose chase." The person who plays this game is one who never updates his files. His records are filled with all sorts of lapsed insurance policies, promissory notes of debts long since paid; brokerage statements of securities that have been sold, and so on.

When he is gone, his family will become frustrated as they try to hunt down the "missing" asset.

If you wish to play this game, then the best joke is to keep the key to a safe deposit box that you are no longer leasing. That will keep folks hunting for a long time!

If you do not have a wicked sense of humor, then do your family a favor and update your records on a regular basis.

Completing The Process 9

The funeral is over.

Everyone went home.

You experienced and got past the initial grief.

All the affairs of the decedent have been settled.

But is the grieving over? Do you have closure? To use a tired expression, have you been able to "get on with your life" or do you find that you are still grieving?

And how about the children in the decedent's life?
How are they taking the loss?

The death event is not over until the family finally finds peace and acceptance of the loss. This book deals with issues that may arise as the family goes through the grieving process.

THE GRIEVING PROCESS

Psychologists have observed that it is common for a person to go through a series of stages as part of the grieving process. There is the initial shock of the death and often disbelief and denial:

"He can't be dead. I just spoke to him today!"

It is common for a mourner to be angry — angry at the decedent for dying — angry at a family member for something he should or shouldn't have done — just plain angry.

Sometimes an ill person is aware of his impending death and becomes angry, as if mourning his own death. Relations with the family may become strained under the stress of the illness. If there was an argument with the decedent, the bereaved may be left with an unresolved conflict and feelings of guilt.

Mourners often experience guilt. Many have an uneasy feeling that the death was somehow their fault. Some regret not having spent more time with the decedent. Others feel guilty because they weren't present when the decedent died.

There is grieving even when death is long expected and even welcomed. This was the case with a wife who nursed her husband at home for nine long years. Her husband suffered from debilitating strokes, a chronic heart condition, and finally failing kidneys. She often said "Some things are worse than death." When he died, she was shocked. He was close to death so many times. Each time he recovered. She couldn't believe he was dead. And she was surprised at the depth of her emotions. She thought she would be relieved. She didn't think she would experience such intense grief.

THE STAGES OF GRIEF

Although professionals in the fields of psychiatry and psychology have observed that guilt and anger are stages of grieving, there is no agreement about the number or composition of the stages of grieving. This is not surprising. The way people react to death is as diverse as there are people. Some people seem not to grieve at all. Whether such people experience any stage of the mourning process may not be known even to the person himself/herself.

And there is diversity in grieving even in the same person. Each circumstance of death in one's life is different from another, so a person will grieve differently when different people in their life die. But for purposes of this discussion, we note that many people who lose someone they love report experiencing the following emotions and in the following sequence:

- initial shock, disbelief, alarm
- numbness, anger, guilt
- an intense longing for the deceased
- sadness, depression, loneliness
- recovery, acceptance of the loss, peace

Very often these emotions are accompanied by physical discomfort:

- tightness in chest, shoulders or throat
- over sensitivity to noise
- breathlessness, causing the person to sigh
- dry mouth
- muscular weakness
- loss of energy, fatigue

COPING WITH THE LOSS

How the general population deals with the death of a loved one was investigated in 1995 by the AMERICAN ASSOCIATION OF RETIRED PERSONS ("AARP"). AARP asked National Communications Research to conduct a telephone survey of over 5,000 people aged 40 or older. Approximately one third of the respondents reported that they had experienced the loss of a close friend or family member within the past year. Those reporting a loss were asked to describe specific coping activities that they had engaged in since the death of their loved one.

- 67% reported talking with friends and family
- 16% read an article or book about how to cope with death
- 9% received help with legal or practical arrangements
- 5% attended a grief support group

When asked what strategies they found to be most helpful in coping with their loss:

- 28% said talking with a friend or family member was most helpful
- 24% said their religion was most helpful
- 10% said knowing it was for the best
- 6% said memories of the deceased
- 4% reported staying busy as the best strategy.

It is interesting to note that 67% of the people who suffered a loss turned to family and friends to help them cope with the loss. Although talking with family and friends topped the list as the most commonly used strategy, only 28% reported this as being most helpful to them. Many times friends and family members want to help but they are at a loss as to what to say or do. The next section discusses different techniques that can be used to help with the grieving process.

HELPING THE BEREAVED

Family and friends want to help the person who is grieving, but sometimes they don't know how to do it. They may feel just as helpless in dealing with the loss as does the bereaved — not knowing what to say to console someone who is grieving.

There are no magic words, but saying you are sorry for the loss is appropriate and generally well received. Avoid platitudes such as: "It was fate." "It was God's will." "It was for the best." Especially avoid telling the bereaved that you know how he/she feels. People who suffer a great loss do not believe that anyone can understand how they feel; and they are probably correct. It is better to tell the bereaved what you are feeling:
"I was shocked when I heard of the death."
"I am so sad for you." "I am going to really miss him."
Knowing that you share the feeling of loss is comforting to someone who is grieving.

The wake or funeral is not the time express curiosity about how property is to be distributed. Statements such as "I gave that imported glass vase to your mother; and I was wondering whether she remembered to tell you to give it to me" are at best tacky, if not downright insensitive.

Listening is more important than talking to the bereaved. They may need to explore the circumstances of the death — how the person died; where and when he died, etc. They may need to express what they are feeling, whether it be grief or anger. Try not to change the subject just because you are uncomfortable with the topic or with the expression of emotion. If the bereaved wishes to reminisce about the decedent, then join in the conversation. Talk about the decedent's good qualities and the enjoyable times that you shared together.

If during the funeral period, you want to do something such as prepare food or send flowers, then consider asking the bereaved for permission to do so. The family may prefer donations to a favorite charity in place of flowers. The family may have already made dinner plans for the guests. Do not make general offers of assistance. "Let me know if you need anything" is not likely to get a response even if the bereaved does need help with something. A better, more sincere, approach is a specific offer, such as, "If you need transportation, I can drive you to the cemetery."

Your assistance during the post-funeral period is more important than during the funeral period. During the funeral the bereaved is usually surrounded by family and friends and has more than ample assistance. Any offer to help at that time may not even register because the bereaved may be numb with grief — unable to comprehend what is going on around them — unable to even recall who was present at the funeral, nonetheless who offered assistance.

Once the funeral is over and everyone has gone home, that is the time to offer support. The bereaved needs to go through a transition period and must learn to live without the presence of their loved one. In general, the more dependent the bereaved was on the decedent, the more difficult the transition. In such case, you can be most helpful if you are able to offer assistance with those tasks of daily living that the bereaved is not accustomed to performing. For example, if the decedent was the sole driver in the family, then you might help the bereaved to learn to drive or at least help find public transportation. If the decedent handled all of the family finances, you might assist the bereaved in bill paying and balancing a checkbook. If math is not your forte, help to find a bookkeeper who can assist for a reasonable fee.

But, the best thing that family and friends can do for the bereaved, is just to be there for them. As shown by the AARP survey, the specific coping activity used by the majority of the bereaved was to talk to a friend or relative. A telephone call or a card on a special anniversary or holiday will be appreciated. You can help most with a call or a visit. It is just that simple.

Also be patient with the bereaved. There is no set time to get through the grieving process. It may take considerable time for the mourner to be able to find some quality of life. If several months have passed and you are concerned that the bereaved is still not functioning well, or at least, better, then you might consider suggesting that the bereaved seek professional counseling. Try not to be judgmental when making the suggestion. Don't say "You should be feeling better by now," but rather, "I can see that you are still having a hard time getting through this difficult period. Have you considered seeing _____?"

Suggest whatever is appropriate to the mourner. For example, if the mourner is a religious person, then suggest a visit with his/her religious leader. If the mourner is a social person, suggest a support group. If the bereaved is severely depressed, a visit to a doctor or psychiatrist may be the best recommendation.

Do not expect your recommendation to be well received. The mourner may become angry or annoyed that you even made the suggestion. It may be difficult for the mourner to accept the fact that he/she needs assistance. Some people, mostly men, think it an admission of weakness to agree that they need help. They believe they should be able to "tough it out."

Some mourners may have increased their consumption of alcohol or turned to drugs in an attempt to deal with the pain that they are experiencing. If they accept your suggestion, they may need to deal with a growing addiction, in addition to the problem of overcoming the grief, and they may not be willing to do that.

Elderly people might think there is a stigma associated with any kind of counseling. They may insist "There's nothing wrong with me" fearing that you think they are unbalanced or somehow mentally defective.

Some people, especially the overachiever type, refuse to seek counseling because they perceive asking for help to be a sign of failure — an admission that they failed to work out the problem themselves. It's as if they failed "Grieving 101."

But those most resistant to a suggestion of a need for counseling are mourners who use denial as a defense mechanism. They may brush off the suggestion with "No. I'm alright" or "I'm doing a lot better." People who deny that they are having trouble getting past the grief, do not want to deal with the problem. If they deny that they have a problem, then they don't have a problem and that solves that!

In such cases, the timeworn adage, "You can lead a horse to water, but you can't make him drink," applies. The mourner needs to take the first step himself. You cannot take it for him. All you can do is assure the mourner (and yourself) that you have confidence that he/she can, and will, work this through.

HELPING A CHILD THROUGH THE LOSS

The first thing parents observe about their second child is how very different that child is from their first child. Parents quickly learn that each of their children is an individual, with his/her own separate response to any given situation. It is important to keep this fact in mind when trying to assist a child through the loss of a close family member or friend. Because each child is different, there is no single proper way to assist a child through a period of mourning. You can help the child most if you consider the child's background as it relates to the loss:

What is the child's relationship to the decedent?
What were the circumstances of the death?
Was it expected or was it sudden or tragic?
What is the emotional age of the child? That age may differ significantly from his/her chronological age.

As an example, consider the family of Harold and Elaine, parents of three children. Emily, the eldest child, was one of those "born old" children, wise beyond her years, sensitive and shy. Her brother John, two years her junior was the direct opposite — boisterous, immature, constantly in motion. Peter came along five years later. He was the baby of the family, a cherub, always smiling, indulged by parents and siblings.

When their paternal grandfather died, Emily was 10, John, 8 and Peter, 3. Their parents expected the death because "Gramps" had been suffering from cancer for a long time. No mention was made to the children of the serious nature of the illness, so Emily was surprised to learn of the death. She shed no tears but retreated to her room and soon became occupied with a computer game.

John and his father cried together when they were told that Gramps had died. Gramps was both kind and generous with a great sense of humor. Best of all he was never critical of John's rambunctious behavior. It seemed to John and his Dad that they lost the best friend they ever had.

Peter did not understand what was going on; but he reacted empathetically, patting John on the shoulder, and saying "Don't cry Johnny."

When it came time to go to the funeral Emily refused to go. Johnny got angry with Emily for something or another and pushed her down. She was not hurt, but she cried loudly and carried on. Peter started whining. The whole day was hard on their parents.

The next few months were equally difficult. John woke up with nightmares. Emily was sullen and withdrawn. No one mentioned the death except Peter who was full of questions: "Where's Gramps?"
"Was he in that box?"
"Where did they put the box?"
"Why was everyone crying?"

Harold and Elaine were having their own problems dealing with the loss and they had no patience with the children. The family eventually got back to normal, but it might have been easier on all of them had the parents prepared the children for the dying process.

PREPARING FOR THE EVENT

Most deaths are expected. The majority of people who die are ill for several months before their death. Children are not always aware of a family member's mortal illness so it comes as a shock to them when it happens. It might have been easier on Emily and John if their parents said something like:

> *Gramps is old and very ill. It happens that all living things, plants, animals and people, eventually die. No one knows for sure when someone will die, but it may be that because he is so old and so very sick that Gramps may die sometime within the year.*

If either child wanted to pursue the subject, then that could lead to a discussion of the funeral process:

> *When someone dies in our family, all of our friends and family gather together to talk about how much we loved the person and how much we will miss having that person with us. Later we go to the gravesite where we say prayers and our last good-byes.*

It is important for parents to explain the children's role in this process, but like most couples, Harold and Elaine never thought about, much less discussed, their children's participation in the funeral and burial service. Had her parents told Emily what to expect and what was expected of her, she might not have objected to attending the funeral.

Before discussing the matter with the child, it is important that a husband and wife explore their own views on their children's participation in a funeral and burial. They may find that they have differing views on the following issues:

What factors should determine whether a child attends the wake and/or funeral:

- ▷ custom or convenience?
- ▷ the age and emotional maturity of that child?
- ▷ the relationship of the child to the decedent?

Should the child be allowed to decide whether he/she wishes to attend the wake and/or funeral?

Should a child be allowed (or encouraged) to touch or kiss the corpse?

Should children participate in grave site ceremonies?

Should a child be encouraged or required to visit the grave site at a later date?

There are no right or wrong answers for any of the above questions. Each family has its own set of customs and values and the answers to these questions need to conform to those customs and values. What is important is that the couple agree about what they expect of their children and then impart that expectation to their children.

The "imparting" is the difficult part. No one likes to talk about death. Parents have been told that they need to discuss sex with their children. They have been told that they need to discuss drugs with their children. These are important, life threatening, issues but it is entirely possible that a child will grow to be an adult without ever having someone close to them die. So why bring up the subject?

The reason to discuss the matter is the same reason to discuss sex with your children. The sex they see on television or hear about from their friends is a reflection of societal values but perhaps not your family values. You discuss sex to impart your values and expectations to your children. If you wish to express your views on the dying process and the afterlife then it is appropriate to discuss these matters when you believe the child is sufficiently mature and ready for the discussion.

An appropriate time for the discussion is when someone close to them is quite aged or seriously ill. If they heard that some family member is dying, they may have concerns or questions that you can answer. Most children fear the unknown and death is an unknown to them. Of course, children are aware of the fact of death almost as soon as they can speak. It is all around them. Animated characters "die" as part of a computer game. Children's cartoon movies and television shows contain death and dying scenes. A child may have a pet that dies. Children hear about people dying almost nightly on the news.

Although children are familiar with the concept of death, they do not know how they or their family will react to the death of a loved one. If the topic is discussed prior to an impending death, the child may find it comforting to know what to expect, what behavior is expected of them, and what choices they may have regarding their attendance at a wake or funeral.

AFTER THE FUNERAL

Once the funeral is over, you need to deal with your own loss. That may be a difficult process for you so you may not even notice that your child is also grieving. This was the case with Harold and Elaine. They were not aware that Emily was having a difficult time with the loss — after all she didn't even cry when she heard of the death. If they thought about it, they may have realized that Emily was retreating into herself as a defense mechanism for dealing with the loss. Her continued sullen attitude after the funeral was a tip off that she was having difficulty getting beyond the loss.

If her parents encouraged Emily to talk about the problem, they would have learned that she had ambivalent feelings about her grandfather. She loved him, but she felt that he favored her brothers. Gramps always played "boy" games of catch and touch football. He never took the time to get to know Emily and she resented that. Now that he was gone, there would be no opportunity for her to have a meaningful relationship with her grandfather.

People are helped most by talking with a friend or relative about their loss. The same applies to children. Emily could have profited had she been able to explore her feelings with either of her parents. Her parents might also have profited because they may have developed a closer relationship with Emily and established a pattern of open communication.

As it was, Emily never did resolve the problem. Her parents suffered her sullenness without ever a clue as to what Emily was all about. Unfortunately, this lack of communication continued as Emily grew older and ever more a closed book.

John fared better. Harold recognized that John's nightmares were related to the loss. Harold made an effort to spend more time with the boy and not to be so critical when John acted up.

As for Peter, his parents tried to answer his questions as best as they were able. Elaine had the uneasy feeling that she was not answering them "the right way." She thought she made a mistake by saying that "Gramps is now at rest" because Peter asked if Gramps was sleeping. She thought that she might have caused Peter to confuse death and sleep.

Had Elaine investigated she could have found any number of excellent publications dealing with the subject. Many funeral homes provide families with complimentary pamphlets on how to answer children's questions about death. The local library and bookstore have any number of excellent publications designed to answer questions raised by small children.

Most religious organizations offer printed material for young people that explain death from the organization's perspective. For religious families, this is a good opportunity for the family to discuss their religious beliefs as they relate to the loss of a loved one.

INTERNET RESOURCES

Many Web sites offer free publications on how to deal with the issues of death and dying. Today's child is computer literate. A child may, on his own, decide to seek an E-mail buddy to work through a problem the child may be having with the death. Parents need to supervise such communication because the child may be especially vulnerable at this point in his/her life.

GriefNet (734) 761-1960
P.O. Box 3272
Ann Arbor, MI 48106-3272

GriefNet offers an E-mail grief support groups. This Web site is operated by Rivendell Resources, a non-profit organization. KIDSAID is a companion Web site to GriefNet. They offer peer support groups for children who are dealing with a loss. Parental permission is required before the child can join a support group.

http://www.griefnet.org/KIDSAID/kidstokids.htm
E-mail: visibility@griefnet.org

TAG: Teen Age Grief, Inc. (661) 253-1932
P.O. Box 220034
Newhall, CA 91322-0034

Teen Age Grief, Inc. is a non-profit organization. Their primary function is to provide expertise in grief support to grieving teens.

http://www.smartlink.net/~tag/
E-mail: tag@smartlink.net

Most deaths are from natural causes. The death is expected and the family is prepared to accept the loss. The ***problem death*** is one that is tragic, unexpected, and/or a death that cuts short a life. School officials understand that the loss of a member of the school community deeply affects the student population. Many schools have adopted a policy of having school psychologists counsel the students as soon as the death occurs. They do not wait until a school child shows signs of being disturbed by the event.

It would be well for parents to adopt the same policy. Specifically, if your family suffers a problem death then consider seeking the services of a professional who is experienced in grief counseling just as soon after the death as is practicable. The next day is none too soon.

A case in point was that of a 14 year old girl who lived with her grandmother, a jovial, robust woman whose main pleasures in life were eating and telling funny stories. One morning when they were eating their usual breakfast of fried eggs, sausage and buttered toast, the grandmother complained about her doctor and how he was on her case about losing weight and lowering her cholesterol. She no sooner finished the sentence when she suffered a heart attack. She died within minutes.

This was a problem death. The death was both unexpected and tragic. Unexpected because the grandmother looked quite healthy. Tragic, because it occurred in the presence of the granddaughter.

No one knew how deeply this affected the girl until a few months had passed. The girl was losing quite a bit of weight. When questioned, she said that it was over-eating that caused her grandmother's death and she wanted to be sure that she ate a healthy diet with absolutely no fat. Concerned family members explained that losing too much weight was just as bad as being overweight. The girl agreed with them, but she continued to lose weight.

When family members realized the severity of the problem they took her to a doctor, who in turn referred them to a psychiatrist. The diagnosis was anorexia. Unfortunately, no amount of therapy, antidepressant, or medical intervention helped. The girl died a year later.

A death does not always need to be a problem death to cause a problem for a child. If a child has unresolved issues with the decedent, then that child may need professional assistance in coping with the loss. Children do not manifest grief or depression in the same way as adults, so look for changes that are atypical of the child and that do not resolve themselves within a reasonable time after the death. Consider consulting with a child psychologist if your child exhibits unusual or antisocial behavior such as:

- eating too much or too little
- destructive or aggressive behavior
- sleeping too much or too little
- misbehaving at school
- a sudden change in school performance

The red flag, signaling an immediate need for counseling, is a child who talks or writes about committing suicide. It is important to act quickly to show the child that you understand that he/she is having a rough time and that you and the doctor want to help the child get through this difficult period.

There are any number of resources in the community to assist the child, from school counselors to religious organizations. The New Jersey Psychological Association, located in Livingston, NJ, can refer you to psychologists in your county who are experienced in grief counseling. Their telephone number is (973) 535-9888.

For those who cannot afford private care, counties offer low-cost services on an ability to pay basis. Some religious organizations offer counseling services to their members, as well as to the general public, on a sliding scale basis.

Before seeking counseling services, it is important to schedule a physical checkup for the child. There is a chance that the problem is physiological. Some illnesses cause behavioral changes; for example, food allergies can cause aggressive behavior. Hearing or visual deficiencies can cause a child to withdraw into himself. Even infections can cause behavioral disturbances. Perhaps the child is on drugs and an examination should pick that up. All these things need to be ruled out prior to counseling.

If your child has been treated by the physician over the years, the doctor may know the child well enough to be able to offer some insight into the problem. If the examination does not reveal a physical problem, the physician may be able to suggest the right type of treatment, i.e., psychologist or psychiatrist, and perhaps give you a referral.

CHOOSING THE RIGHT COUNSELOR

There was a film called GOOD WILL HUNTING in which a brilliant, but troubled, teenager was required, by court order, to attend counseling. The funniest part of the film was the manner in which the boy went through counselors. He deliberately alienated (and was alienated) by many doctors until he met the right one for him. Similarly, if your child needs counseling you might need to interview several counselors before you find someone with whom your child can work; someone who speaks on his/her level — someone the child can trust.

The issue of trust may create a dilemma for the parent. The child is the counselor's patient. The counselor cannot betray the child's trust by revealing what was said during treatment, yet parents need to know whether the treatment is helping the child. The counselor can, and should, disclose to the parent the diagnosis, prognosis and type of proposed treatment. The parents need to employ someone they trust to pursue the course of treatment that they determine is best for their child.

In seeking a counselor, personal references are the best avenue. With or without references, you need to investigate the counselor's background. What is his/her training? What percentage of the practice is devoted to grief counseling children in this age group? Interview more than one counselor before making your choice. If the child is sufficiently mature and able to cooperate in choosing the right counselor, then that is an important step forward. If not, you may need to be assertive and go with the counselor whom you trust and are most comfortable. If it turns out that there is no improvement within a few months, then you need to find another counselor. As with the student in GOOD WILL HUNTING, it may take several tries before you come upon someone who can help your child.

THE ADULT ORPHAN

The baby boomers are a unique group in many ways. What other group has transition periods marked by headlines? "Baby Boomers Turn 50" is the latest newsworthy event. The "Adult Orphan" is a condition unique to that age group. Most Boomers have had their parents with them for half a century. Their parents have survived longer than any other generation in recorded history. But now the Boomers' parents are in their 80s and 90s and Boomers will need to learn to live without them.

Many have functioned independently for years and can handle the loss without problem. For others it is overwhelming. That was the case with two sisters. Opposites from birth. Patti was an independent spirit. Rebellious, strong-willed, she left her hometown to go to college and never looked back. She didn't even resemble her sister Maria. Maria was short, dark-haired, with a bit of a weight problem. Patti looked like an aging flower child with long, straight hair. You'd hardly pick them out as sisters, except for the fact of the resemblance to their parents. Patti had her Dad's angular features (especially his sharp nose), and Maria, her mother's round face and large dark eyes.

Maria lived within 10 miles of her parents all her life. It was a great shock when her Dad died suddenly of a heart attack. But her mother was there to comfort her and offer her words of encouragement, even though her Mom was struggling with the loss herself. That was the way Mom was. Always putting the needs of her children before her own. Patti was the strong one at Dad's funeral. Making funeral arrangements. Greeting family members. Helping Mom to settle Dad's estate. She seemed to know exactly what needed to be done and how to do it.

Maria seemed as dependent as Patti was independent. Maybe it was Maria's personality. Maybe she was raised that way. Maybe her parents needed Maria to need them as much as Maria needed to lean on them.
"Co-dependent" taunted Patti.
How Maria hated that phrase!

Maria never thought of herself as being dependent. She married and raised two children of her own. Over the last few years she took care of her mother as her mother's health failed. Maria's whole day revolved around her mother. Making sure she was fed and comfortable. Maria did not know what she would do with all her time now that her role of caretaker was done. But the emotional loss was the hardest part. Her mother had been her closest confident, her best friend.

Maria held up better at the funeral than she had expected. It was Patti who seemed to fall apart. When Maria thought about it, she understood. Her parents gave Patti unconditional love. Patti found that nowhere else. All other relationships in her life were flawed. Her two marriages ended in divorce and that bothered her greatly. Bad enough to make a mistake once. How could she have been so stupid as to pick two losers? Yet her parents neither condemned nor criticized. They were there for Patti emotionally and financially. They were her safety net. Now they were both gone.

At the funeral Maria looked over at Patti. She seemed lost, like a motherless child, an orphan. Now Patti would need to grow old without her parents. Now she would need to grow up.

STRATEGIES TO COPE WITH THE LOSS

Once a person accepts the fact of death, they are past the initial phase of the grief process. Most people do very well and are able to go through the remaining stages with no overt effort on their part. Others suffer profoundly and need to find ways to get through the grieving process. If you have recently experienced a loss and are having difficulty coping with the loss then consider your own personality type and explore those strategies that might help you through.

Do you enjoy socializing with people or do you prefer solitary activities? Are you a "do-it-yourself" type of person or do you feel more at ease with someone leading you through the process?

STRATEGIES FOR THE PRIVATE PERSON

If you find socializing to be difficult, then consider non-social activities such as reading a self help book. There are many excellent publications that explore the grieving process and how to adjust to the loss. Praying or quiet meditation may offer you consolation. This may be a good time to explore different kinds of meditative techniques. You can find books on meditative techniques such as Zen or visualization in the Philosophy section of the library or bookstore. You can find books on Yoga in the exercise section.

If you are computer literate, you can use your browser to locate an Internet support group. An anonymous friend may be the perfect confidant to help you to work through the sadness and loneliness that you are feeling. You can locate E-mail support groups for people who are dealing with all types of grief issues by searching the following topics: GRIEF MOURNING DEATH DYING

STRATEGIES FOR THE SOCIAL MINDED

If you are a social person, consider using those types of activities that involve a social setting, such as joining a bridge club, bowling or golfing group. If your grief is too deep to concentrate on recreational activities, consider joining a support group. The power of the support group is companionship. They offer the one thing you may need most at this time — just someone to listen.

If you belong to an organized religion or a civic organization, find out whether they have a support group for people who are going through the grieving process. If your organization does not have a support group, consider starting one yourself. It can be as simple as putting a notice in a weekly bulletin that you are holding a meeting for anyone who lost a loved one within the past year. You can hold the meeting as part of a picnic or barbecue with everyone bringing a dish for others to share. Just getting together and sharing experiences may help you and others in your organization as well.

If you do not belong to an organization, look in the newspaper for notices of meetings of local support groups or consider joining one of the many national support groups. The following are some of the well established national groups:

FOR WIDOWED PERSONS

AARP GRIEF AND LOSS PROGRAM
WIDOWED PERSONS SERVICE (800) 424-3410
601 E Street NW
Washington, DC 20049

AARP has support groups for widowed persons throughout the United States. They also have support groups for adults who have suffered the loss of a family member such as a parent or sibling. You can call the above 800 number and they will let you know if there is a support group in your area.

E-mail: griefandloss@ aarp.org
Web site: www.aarp.org/griefprograms

THEOS (412) 471-7779
(**T**hey **H**elp **E**ach **O**ther **S**piritually)
322 Boulevard of the Allies, Suite 105
Pittsburgh, PA 15222-1919

THEOS is a national organization with a volunteer network of recently widowed persons. They have support chapters in many states. If you wish to establish a support group in your area, they will help you to do so.

FOR WIDOWED PARENTS

PARENTS WITHOUT PARTNERS (800) 637-7974
401 N. Michigan Avenue
Chicago, IL 60611-6267

PARENTS WITHOUT PARTNERS is a national non-profit organization for single parents. They offer group discussions and single parent activities such as picnics and hikes. Their national headquarters in Illinois can direct you to the chapter nearest you.

PARENTS WITHOUT PARTNERS WEB SITE
http://parentswithoutpartners.org
E-mail: pwp@jti.com

PET GRIEF SUPPORT SERVICES

Those who suffer the loss of a pet may experience a sense of loss similar to the loss of a close family member. Often they hesitate to turn to friends or family members (especially those who never owned a pet) believing they just wouldn't understand.

Some local Humane Societies provide a pet loss counseling service. Some veterinarian medical schools have volunteer counseling services.

There is a list of pet grief counseling services for other states at
http://www.superdog.com/

THE PHYSICAL ASPECTS OF GRIEVING

As discussed, accompanying the emotional stages of grief, are physical symptoms that mourners commonly experience, such as tightness in the chest; muscular weakness; loss of energy and fatigue.

It is just as important to deal with the physical aspects of grieving as it is with the emotional. People who suffer extreme grief tend to become extreme in everyday activities. They may forget to eat. Some find themselves eating all day. Some mourners develop sleep disturbances and go without sleep for long periods of time while others suffer the opposite extreme of wanting to sleep all day. If you find that your grief is affecting your physical wellbeing, then you need to make a conscious effort to care for yourself:

✯ EAT A BALANCED NUTRITIONAL DIET

Contrary to popular taste, sugar, salt, fat and chocolate do not constitute the four basic food groups. And contrary to current food faddism, no one diet fits all. The ability to digest certain foods varies from person to person and we all have ethnic preferences. You need to learn what balance of fats, protein (meat, fish, legumes) and carbohydrates (fruit, vegetables, grains) you require to maintain your optimum weight and state of well being; and then make an effort to keep that balance in your daily diet.

✯ GET SUFFICIENT REST

There is much variation in the amount of sleep required from person to person. You know how much sleep you normally require. Try to maintain your usual, pre-loss, sleep pattern. If you are finding difficulty sleeping at night, resist the urge to sleep during the day. It is easy to reverse your days and nights. Awake all night, dozing all day, will only make you feel as if you are walking around in a fog.

✯ EXERCISE EACH DAY

Exercise can be as simple as taking a brisk 20 minute walk, however the more sustained and energetic, the greater the benefit. If you are having trouble sleeping at night, try exercising during the late afternoon and eating your main meal at lunch rather than late at night.

Eating right, getting sufficient sleep, exercising — most people have heard these recommendations from so many sources (doctors, psychologists, writers for health magazines, etc.) that they seem to have become a cliche. But the reason that so many professionals make these suggestions is simply that they work. Doing all these things should make you feel significantly better.

And this may be the time for a complete physical checkup. Grieving is hard on the body. The cause of your physical discomfort may not emotional. It could be that there is a medical problem that needs attending.

ADJUSTING TO A NEW LIFE STYLE

If you lost a member of your immediate family, then in addition to going through the stages of the grieving process, you need to go through a transition period in which you learn how to live without the decedent. The child must learn to live without the guidance of a parent. Parents may need to put their parenting behind them. The spouse must learn to live without a partner, and as a single person.

In addition to learning to live with the loss, the bereaved may need to establish a new identity. Such was the case with Claire. She and Fred were married 44 years when he died after a lengthy battle with cancer. At first Claire didn't think she could live without him. She had been a wife for so long. She had trouble thinking of herself as a single person — nonetheless being one.

Claire had difficulty accepting the fact that Fred was dead, even though she expected he would die for months before he did. She would see Fred in her dreams. Sometimes she thought she saw him sitting in his favorite chair. When Fred appeared to Claire, he looked the same as when they were first married. Sometimes she thought he was speaking to her.

What was most comforting to Claire was that Fred was smiling at her. She was relieved to know that Fred was no longer in pain and was at peace. The smile on his face was a relief to her because she feared he might be angry with her for the many times he would call out her name and she would become annoyed with him. She felt guilty that she did not have more patience as a caregiver.

Claire found herself talking to Fred especially during those times that she was undecided as to what to do. As time progressed, she began to incorporate her husband's beliefs into her own so that instead of asking herself "What should I do?" it became "This is what Fred would have done."

Eventually Claire found that she was able to function on her own. She began to re-engage with the world. She found new interests to pleasantly occupy her time. She learned how to live as a single person. She is now more self sufficient than at any other time in her life. She laments that Fred no longer visits her. She still misses him.

Claire was able to get beyond the grief. She did it on her own, though she will tell you that she did it with Fred's help.

Claire's case is not unusual. As verified by the AARP survey, most people adjust to the loss on their own, requiring only an assist from family and friends, but there is a percentage of the grieving population that will require assistance and need to seek professional grief counseling.

For those experiencing psychological problems prior to the death, the event of the death may be the precipitating factor to mental illness requiring treatment. Similarly, if a person had a drinking problem or a drug addiction before the death, the event of the death may exacerbate the addiction.

Some deaths are so violent or tragic, that even the sturdiest may be unable to resume their life without professional assistance. In the next section, we discuss ways of coping with the problem death.

THE PROBLEM DEATH

As discussed, the problem death is one that is unexpected, tragic or a death that cuts short a life. Such a death is an immediate problem in terms of the funeral, burial and estate settlement, but the most difficult problem is getting through the mourning period.

The death of a child is always a problem death. Even if the child is an adult, the parent experiences extreme grief. No one expects to outlive his or her child. In these days of a lengthening life cycle, more and more parents may come to experience such a loss. The loss may come at a time when the parent is frail or in poor health, making it all the more difficult to deal with the loss.

The only thing harder than losing an adult child is losing a young child. Nothing compares to the intensity of grief experienced by a parent when a little one dies. Some parents believe they are losing their mind. Many feel that their lives can never have meaning again. Guilt and recrimination flow, "Maybe I could have prevented it." There is even guilt for returning to ordinary living. If the parents find themselves smiling, laughing or making love they think, "How can we be doing this? How can we ever be normal again?"

The family who experiences a tragic or violent death should consider seeking professional grief counseling as soon as practicable after the death. The grief counseling can be in the format of a self-help group. Participants are able to talk and share their pain with others like themselves who understand what they are experiencing.

There are many specialized self-help groups that provide literature and peer support for families who experience a problem death.

FOR PRENATAL OR NEONATAL DEATHS

M.E.N.D. **M**ommies **E**nduring **N**eonatal **D**eath
P.O. Box 1007 (888)-695-MEND
Coppell, TX 75019

MEND provides monthly newsletters and has a Web site that with information:.

http://www.mend.org
E-mail rebekah@mend.org

SHARE (800) 821-6819
National Share Pregnancy and Infant Loss Support
St. Joseph Health Center
300 First Capitol Drive
St. Charles, MO 63301-2893

SHARE is a resource center for bereaved parents. They have support groups throughout the United States. You can call the national office for the telephone number of the support group in your state.

http://www.nationalshareoffice.com
E-mail share@nationalshareoffice.com

FOR FAMILIES OF A DECEASED CHILD

THE COMPASSIONATE FRIENDS
National Chapter: (630) 990-0010
P.O. Box 3696, Oak Brook, IL 60522
THE COMPASSIONATE FRIENDS have local chapters with volunteers (themselves bereaved parents) to accept telephone calls.

http://www.compassionatefriends.org
E-mail: nationaloffice@compassionatefriends.org

A.G.A.S.T (888) 774-7437
ALLIANCE OF **G**RANDPARENTS **A** **S**UPPORT IN **T**RAGEDY
P.O. Box 17281
Phoenix, AZ 85011-0281
AGAST supports grandparents, who have suffered the loss of a grandchild, with informational packets, peer contact and newsletters.

E-mail: GRANMASIDS@AOL.COM

SIDS ALLIANCE (800) 221-7437
SUDDEN INFANT DEATH SYNDROME ALLIANCE
1314 Bedford Avenue, Suite 210
Baltimore, MD 21208

The SIDS Alliance is a national, not-for-profit, voluntary organization. Their Web site offers information and the names and E-mail addresses of chapters in all of the states.

http//www.sidsalliance.org
E-mail: sidshg@charm.net

FOR FAMILIES OF MURDERED CHILDREN

THE NATIONAL ORGANIZATION OF (888) 818-POMC
PARENTS **O**F **M**URDERED **C**HILDREN, INC.
National Chapter
100 East Eighth Street, B-41
Cincinnati, OH 45202

POMC has support groups and contact people in each of the fifty states. You can contact the National Chapter for the group nearest you.

http://www.pomc.com
E-mail natlpomc@aol.com

FOR FAMILIES OF SUICIDES

AMERICAN ASSOC. OF SUICIDOLOGY (202) 237-2280
4201 Connecticut Ave. NW, Suite 408
Washington, DC 20008

The American Association of Suicidology is a not-for-profit organization that promotes education, public awareness and research for suicide prevention. It serves as a national clearinghouse for information on suicide. You can call for the number of a support group nearest you. Their Web site has the names addresses and phone number of several organizations that offer counseling for families who have lost a loved one to suicide.

http://www.suicidology.org

BUT WHAT IF I CAN'T STOP GRIEVING?

We observed that there are five stages of grieving:

shock/disbelief
anger/guilt
searching/pining
sadness/depression
acceptance of the loss.

There is no right way to grieve. You may pass through a stage rapidly or even skip a stage. You may get hung up in one of the stages and have difficulty getting beyond that emotion. Some psychologists refer to this as "stuckness." It's something like what happened to 45-rpm phonograph records that were popular in the 1940's and 1950's.

For the benefit of the digital generation who have no experience with phonographs, the record was played by means of a needle that glided over groves of a revolving disk (the record). Sometimes the needle would get stuck in a groove and play the same sound over and over again until the annoyed listener bumped it into the next groove.

If you are stuck in one of the stages of mourning you may think the suggestions in this section to be useless in your situation because they encourage you to be proactive, i.e., to actively seek to help yourself. If you are thinking:

"I **can't** help myself. " or

"If I could help myself, I wouldn't have this problem," then the first thing you need to understand, and accept, is that you have no other choice but to help yourself. The pain exists within you and nowhere else. Because the pain is internal and unique to you, only you can ease that pain. This does not mean that no one can help you to deal with the pain. It just means that you need to be interactive with the healing process; and in particular, you need to take the first step.

What is that first step? To answer that question you need to identify those areas of your life with which you are having difficulty. It might help to make a list of all of the things that are bothering you. Once you compose the list, look at the last item on the list. If you are like most people, you will initially avoid thinking about what is really troubling you. It may take the last item on the list for you to admit to yourself what is really causing the problem.

Once you identify the problem, the identification itself should suggest the solution. For example, suppose you find the holidays unbearable, then a solution may be to change your holiday routine. Instead of wearing yourself out shopping for gifts, use the money to treat yourself to a boat cruise. Tell everyone that this year you are taking a holiday from the holidays. You may find that people are just as tired of exchanging gifts as you are and that they gladly welcome the change.

If your problem is being lonely, then your solution will involve companionship. How you find companionship depends on your personality. If you are lonely, but not a social person, consider adopting a pet. If you are civic minded, then you may find companionship as a volunteer for community activities. If you are physically active, perhaps you can take up a new sport or even pick up a sport that you used to enjoy at an earlier time in your life. If you enjoy sports but are not in the best shape, perhaps you can coach children's team sports.

If your problem is that you are severely depressed, the solution will involve medical and/or psychological methods of lifting the depression. If you decide to ask for medical assistance, you need to continue to be interactive. You cannot stand passively by saying "Now heal me." Pharmaceutical hyperbole notwithstanding, there is no magic pill. An antidepressant may help you to gain control of yourself, but you still need to work through the grief.

Make an effort to concentrate on things in your life that are right, as opposed to thoughts that make you angry or sad. This may be difficult to do. During periods of high stress, you may feel as if your mind has a mind of its own. Thoughts may race through your mind even though you'd just as soon not think them. Prayer and/or meditation may help you to reestablish discipline in your thinking process.

If you feel that you have tried it all and you still are unable to find peace and contentment in your life, you need to ask the hard question:

"What is it about mourning that I really enjoy?"

Strange question?

Not really.

You may enjoy thinking of your loved one even if the thought gives you as much pain as pleasure. You may think that if you stop mourning then you truly lose the decedent. If that's the case, then compartmentalize your grief, that is, set aside a special time of the day to actively think about and/or grieve for your loved one and the rest of the day not to grieve or even think about the decedent.

Actively plan the grieving compartment of your day. You may wish to have a grieving routine, perhaps visit the grave site once a week; or quietly spend 15 minutes a day looking at pictures of the decedent or writing down your memories of the happy times you had together. If you have been discussing your grief with family or friends, restrict such talks to specific times, perhaps on the decedent's birthday, or on the anniversary of his death.

Set aside as much time each day as you believe you need to mourn, but here is the hard part — you need to exercise self restraint not to mourn, nor talk about, nor even think of the decedent during any other part of the day. If your mind wanders back to the sadness and loneliness of the loss, postpone it. Say to yourself, "Hold that thought till my next grieving compartment."

If you are speaking to someone, do not mention the decedent or how you are feeling about the loss until your scheduled grieving talk with that person. If the subject comes up during a conversation, then change the subject by saying "We'll talk about that later."

Hopefully you will find the pain of your loss to lessen over time, in frequency and/or intensity.

It isn't so much that time heals; it is more that you learn to heal yourself over time.

Glossary

ADMINISTRATION The ***administration*** of a Probate Estate is the management and settlement of the decedent's affairs. There are different types of administration. See ***Ancillary Administration.***

ADVANCE HEALTH CARE DIRECTIVE An ***Advance Health Care Directive*** is a statement made by someone (the principal) in the presence of witnesses or a written, notarized statement in which the principal gives directions about the care he/she wishes to receive. See ***Living Will***.

AFFIANT An ***affiant*** is someone who signs an affidavit and swears that it is true in the presence of a Notary Public or other person with authority to administer an oath.

AFFIDAVIT An ***affidavit*** is a written statement of fact made by someone voluntarily and under oath, in the presence of a notary public or someone else who has authority to administer an oath.

ANATOMICAL GIFT An ***anatomical gift*** is the donation of all or part of the body of the decedent for a specified purpose, such as transplantation or research.

ANCILLARY ADMINISTRATION An ***ancillary administration*** is a probate procedure that aids or assists the original (primary) probate proceeding. Ancillary administration is conducted in another state to determine the beneficiary of the decedent's property located within that state.

ANNUITANT An ***annuitant*** is someone who is entitled to receive payments under an annuity contract.

ANNUITY An ***annuity*** is a contract that gives someone (the annuitant) the right to receive periodic payments (monthly, quarterly) either for life or for a number of years.

ASSET An ***asset*** is anything owned by someone that has a value, including personal property (jewelry, paintings, securities, cash, motor vehicles, etc.) and real property (condominiums, vacant lots, acreage, residences, etc.)

ATTESTING WITNESS: An ***attesting witness*** to a Will is someone who signs the Will, at the request of and in the presence of the person making the Will, for the purpose of proving that the person who made the Will did sign it, and did so on his own free will.

BENEFICIARY A ***beneficiary*** is one who benefits from the acts of another person. In this book, we refer to a beneficiary as one who inherits a gift from the decedent.

CLAIM A ***claim*** against the decedent's estate is a demand for payment of the debt of the decedent. To be effective, the claim must be filed with the Probate court within the time limits set by law.

CODICIL A ***codicil*** to a Will is an addition to a Will that changes certain parts of the Will.

COLUMBARIUM A ***columbarium*** is a vault with niches (spaces) for urns that contain the ashes of cremated bodies.

CONSERVATOR In New Jersey, a ***conservator*** is someone appointed by the Surrogate's Court to take care of the person and property of someone who is incapacitated because of age or infirmity.

COMMON LAW MARRIAGE A ***common law marriage*** is one that is entered into without a state marriage license or any kind of official marriage ceremony. A common law marriage is created by an agreement to marry, followed by the two living together as man and wife. Most states do not recognize a common law marriage as being a valid marriage.

COURT The ***Court*** as used in this book is the Probate Court. When referring to an order made by the Court, the term is synonymous with "Judge," i.e., an "order of the Court" is an order made by the Judge of the Probate Court.

CREMAINS The word ***cremains*** is an abbreviation of the term ***cremated remains***. It refers to the ***ashes*** of a person who has been cremated.

DECEDENT The ***decedent*** is the person who died.

DISTRIBUTION The ***distribution*** of a trust estate or of a Probate Estate is the delivering to the beneficiary that part of the estate to which the beneficiary is entitled.

DOWER ***Dower*** is the right of a widow to a life estate in one third of all real property owned by her husband at any time during the course of their marriage. This English Common Law has been abolished by most states.

ESTATE A person's ***Estate*** is all of the property (both real and personal property) owned by that person. The decedent's estate may also be referred to as his ***Taxable Estate*** because all of the decedent's assets must be included when determining whether any Estate taxes are due after the person dies. Compare to Probate Estate.

FIDUCIARY A ***fiduciary*** is one who holds property in trust for another or one who acts for the benefit of another.

GRANTEE The ***grantee*** of a deed (also called the party of the second part) named in a deed is the person who receives title to the property from the grantor.

GRANTOR A ***Grantor*** is someone who transfers property. The grantor of a deed, is the person who transfers property to a new owner (the ***Grantee***). The grantor of a trust is someone who creates the trust and then transfers property into the trust. See ***Settlor*** and ***Trustor***.

GUARDIAN In New Jersey, a ***guardian*** is someone appointed by the Surrogate's Court to care for the person and/or property of a minor child.

HEALTH CARE REPRESENTATIVE A ***Health Care Representative*** is a person appointed by someone (the principal) to make health care decisions for the Principal in the event that the Principal is too ill to speak for himself.

HEIR An ***heir*** is someone who is entitled to inherit the decedent's property in the event that the decedent dies intestate (without a Will). This includes the surviving spouse and the state of New Jersey, if the decedent had no surviving relative.

HOMESTEAD The ***homestead*** is the dwelling and land owned and occupied as the owner's principal residence.

INDIGENT A person who is ***indigent*** is one who is poor, destitute and without funds.

INTESTATE ***Intestate*** means not having a Will or dying without a Will. ***Testate*** is to have a Will or dying with a Will.

IRREVOCABLE CONTRACT An ***irrevocable contract*** is a contract that cannot be revoked, withdrawn, or cancelled by any of the parties to that contract.

KEY MAN INSURANCE ***Key man insurance*** is an insurance policy designed to protect a company from economic loss in the event that an important employee of the company becomes disabled or dies.

LEGALESE ***Legalese*** refers to legal terms and confusing text used by some attorneys to draft legal documents.

LETTERS OF ADMINISTRATION ***Letters of Administration*** is a document, issued by the Probate court, giving the person who is appointed as Administrator, authority to take possession of and to administer the estate of the decedent.

LETTERS TESTAMENTARY ***Letters Testamentary*** is a document given to the person who is the Executor of the decedent's Will that gives the Executor authority to take possession of and to administer the estate of the decedent.

LIFE ESTATE A ***life estate*** interest in real property is the right to possess and occupy that property for so long as the holder of the life estate lives.

LINEAL DESCENDANT A ***lineal descendant*** of the decedent is someone who is his direct descendant, such as his child, grandchild, great-grandchild etc.

LITIGATION ***Litigation*** is the process of carrying on a lawsuit, i.e., to sue for some right or remedy in a court of law.

LIVING WILL A ***Living Will*** is a Health Care Directive that gives instructions about whether life support systems should be withheld in the event that the person who signs the Living Will is terminally ill or in a persistent vegetative state and unable to speak for himself.

MEDICAID ***Medicaid*** is a public assistance program sponsored jointly by the federal and state government to provide medical care for people with low income.

NET PROCEEDS The ***net proceeds*** of a sale is the sale price less costs and expenses paid to make the sale.

NET WORTH A person's ***net worth*** is the value of all of the property that he owns less the monies he owes.

NEXT OF KIN ***Next of kin*** has two meanings in law: ***next of kin*** can refer to a person's nearest blood relation or it can refer to those people (not necessarily blood relations) who are entitled to inherit the property of the decedent if the decedent died without a will.

PERJURY ***Perjury*** is lying under oath. The false statement can be made as a witness in court or by signing a false Affidavit. Perjury is a criminal offense.

PERSONAL PROPERTY ***Personal property*** is all property owned by a person that is not real property (real estate). It includes cars, stocks, house furnishings, jewelry, etc. Personal property is sometimes called ***personalty***.

PERSONAL REPRESENTATIVE The ***Personal Representative*** is someone appointed by the Surrogate's court to settle the decedent's estate and to distribute whatever is left to the proper beneficiary.

PER STIRPES GIFT A ***per stirpes*** gift is a gift which is given to a group of people such that if one of them dies before the gift is made, then that deceased person's share goes to his/her lineal descendants.

POWER OF ATTORNEY A ***Power of Attorney*** is a document that appoints an Agent to act for or on behalf of the person who signs the document (the Principal). The Power of Attorney states those things that the Agent can do on behalf of his Principal.

PRE-NUPTIAL AGREEMENT A ***pre-nuptial agreement*** (also known as an ***antenuptial agreement***) is an agreement made prior to marriage whereby a couple determines how their property is to be managed during their marriage and how their property is to be divided should one die, or they later divorce.

PROBATE ***Probate*** is a court procedure in which a court determines the existence of a valid Will and then supervises the distribution of the Probate Estate of the decedent. In the absence of a valid Will, the court determines the proper heirs according to state law of Intestate Succession and oversees the Administration of the estate.

PROBATE ESTATE The ***Probate Estate*** is that part of the decedent's estate that is subject to probate. It includes property that the decedent owned in his name only. It does not include property that was jointly held by the decedent and someone else. It does not include property held "in trust for" or "for the benefit of" someone.

REAL PROPERTY ***Real property,*** also known as ***real estate,*** is land and anything permanently attached to the land such as buildings and fences.

REGISTERED AGENT A ***Registered Agent*** of a corporation is someone who is authorized to act on behalf of the company and accept service of process in the event the company is sued.

REPARATION ***Reparation*** is money paid to make up for an injury or wrongdoing.

RESIDUARY BENEFICIARY A ***residuary beneficiary*** is a beneficiary named in a Will who is entitled to whatever is left of the Probate Estate once the specific gifts made in the Will have been distributed and once the decedent's bills, taxes and costs of probate have been paid. If there is more than one residuary beneficiary, then they share equally in the residuary estate.

RESIDUARY ESTATE A ***residuary estate*** is that part of a probate estate that is left after all expenses and costs of administration have been paid and specific gifts have been distributed.

SETTLOR A ***Settlor*** is someone who furnishes property that is placed in a trust. If the Settlor is also the creator of the trust, then the settlor is also referred to as the Grantor or Trustor.

SPENDTHRIFT TRUST A ***Spendthrift Trust*** is a trust created to provide monies to a beneficiary, and at the same time protect the beneficiary from the monies from being taken by the his creditors.

STATUTE OF LIMITATION A ***statute of limitation*** is a federal or state law that sets maximum time periods for taking legal action. Once the time set out in the statute passes, no legal action can be taken.

SURETY ON A BOND The ***surety on a bond*** for probate procedures is usually an insurance company who will guarantee to pay the beneficiaries of the estate any loss they suffer as a result of the failure of the Decedent's Representative to do his job properly.

SURROGATE A ***surrogate*** is a substitute; someone who acts in place of another.

SURROGATE'S COURT In New Jersey, the Surrogate's Court and the Superior Court handles probate and guardianship procedures.

TANGIBLE PERSONAL PROPERTY ***Tangible Personal Property*** is personal property that can be touched, such as jewelry, a camera, a computer, a record collection, etc.

TENANCY BY THE ENTIRETY A ***Tenancy by the Entirety*** is the name of a form of ownership of real property held by a husband and wife. It has the same legal effect as a joint tenancy with right of survivorship.

TENANCY IN COMMON ***Tenancy in common*** is a form of ownership such that each tenant owns his/her share without any claim to that share by the other tenants. Unlike a joint tenancy, there is no right of survivorship. Once a tenant in common dies, his/her share belongs to the tenant's estate and not to the remaining owners of the property.

TESTATE ***Testate*** means having a Will or dying with a Will.

TITLE INSURANCE ***Title Insurance*** is a policy issued by a title company after searching title to the property. The policy insures the accuracy of the title search against a claim of a defective title.

TRUSTEE A ***Trustee*** is a person, or institution, who accepts the duty of caring for property for the benefit of another.

TRUST AGREEMENT A ***trust agreement*** is document in which someone (the Grantor or Trustor) creates a trust and appoints a trustee to manage property placed into the trust. The usual purpose of the trust is to benefit persons or charities named by the Grantor as beneficiaries of the trust.

TRUSTOR The ***Trustor*** is the creator of a trust.

UNDUE INFLUENCE ***Undue influence*** is pressure or persuasion that overpowers a person's free will so that the dominated person is not acting intelligently or voluntarily.

WAIVER A ***waiver*** is the intentional and voluntary giving up of a known right.

WARRANTY DEED A ***warranty deed*** is a deed in which someone (the Grantor) transfers the property to another (the Grantee) and guarantees good title, i.e., the Grantor guarantees that he has the right to transfer the property, and that no one else has any right to the property.

INDEX

C

J

K

L

T

162 New Jersey Statutes are referenced in
Guiding Those Left Behind In New Jersey

Each state has its own set of laws relating to the settlement of a person's estate. The Ohio laws that are referenced in this book are very different from the laws of other states. The author is in now in the process of "translating" *Guiding Those Left Behind . . .* for the rest of the states; that is, to write a book that incorporates the laws of the state into a book that describes how to settle the affairs of a decedent in that state, and how to prepare an estate plan that is appropriate for the state.

Arizona, California, Florida, Illinois, New Jersey, New York, North Carolina, Ohio, Pennsylvania and Texas are now in print. The following books are scheduled for release by January, 2001:

Guiding Those Left Behind In Georgia
Guiding Those Left Behind In Massachusetts
Guiding Those Left Behind In Michigan
Guiding Those Left Behind In Virginia

The following books are scheduled for release by April 2001:

Guiding Those Left Behind in Indiana
Guiding Those Left Behind In Maryland
Guiding Those Left Behind In Missouri
Guiding Those Left Behind in Washington

To order a book call (800) 824-0823.
Visit our Web site http://www.eaglepublishing.com to check whether books from other states are available at this time.